Talking about Sonatas

ANTONY HOPKINS
After an introductory discussion of how
the concerto form developed, Antony
Hopkins analyses eleven concertos,
including two for piano by Mozart, two
piano concertos and the violin concerto
by Beethoven, two works by Brahms,
and one each by Schumann, Dvorak,
and Rachmaninoff. The final chapter
deals with Bartok's Concerto for
orchestra.

ANTONY HOPKINS

Talking about

SONATAS

A book of analytical studies,
based on a personal view

HEINEMANN
LONDON

Heinemann Educational Books Ltd
LONDON MELBOURNE EDINBURGH TORONTO
JOHANNESBURG AUCKLAND NEW DELHI
HONG KONG NAIROBI
SINGAPORE IBADAN

ISBN 0 435 81425 7 (cased)
0 435 81426 5 (paperback)

First Published 1971

Published by
Heinemann Educational Books Ltd
48 Charles Street, London W1X 8AH
Printed in Great Britain by
William Clowes & Sons Limited
London, Beccles and Colchester

CONTENTS

5

NOTE

It is impossible in writing a book of this nature to gauge accurately just how much the reader already knows. If I have, at times, wasted space on fairly elementary matters like key relationships, I ask the knowledgeable reader to be indulgent; if at other times I have assumed too much, I would remind the less-informed that there are many excellent books on the rudiments of music which will clear up any obscurities.

A.H.

This book was to have been dedicated to Arthur Langford, who for a number of years produced my talks at the B.B.C. Sadly, he died just as it was going to press, and so, although he knew it was on the way, he never saw the finished version. My gratitude to him remains.

ILLUSTRATIONS

The diagrams and musical examples
have been drawn by John Barkwith.

CHAPTER I

A MATTER OF FORM

THE WORD SONATA embraces so many different types of
composition, of such infinitely varied proportions, that it
has become virtually meaningless as a definition. There are sonatas
for piano, for piano and another instrument (ranging from flute
to trombone and including all the members of the string family),
sonatas for solo violin, solo cello, for string orchestra, for organ,
and even one unique example, by Medtner, for voice and piano.
Evolution in music moves at a very much quicker rate than it does
in the animal kingdom; the transition from the crab-like trilobite
which was the earliest known life-form to the giant dinosaurs
took many millions of years. While it might seem discourteous
to both composers to pursue the analogy too far, nevertheless,
there is nearly as wide a gulf between one of the briefer keyboard
sonatas of Scarlatti and the third piano sonata of Brahms; this
evolutionary process took a mere century and a quarter. In this
short period of time, the sonata emerged as the most important
musical form, and rose to a supremacy so total that it became the
framework of every large musical structure, whether for orchestra,
soloist and orchestra, a small group of players or a single performer.
What are symphonies but sonatas for orchestra, what are concertos
but sonatas for a soloist and orchestra, what are quartets but
sonatas for four instruments? If I equate Brahms' third piano
sonata with a dinosaur, it is not entirely irreverent, nor facetious.
The dinosaur must have been an awe-inspiring and wonderful
creature, and those are both adjectives which I would readily
apply to Brahms' magnificent work. But as with the dinosaur,
sheer magnitude leads to obsolescence, and while the Brahms
piano sonatas are the logical outcome of a line of progression
stretching back for over one hundred years, they also mark a
point at which composers instinctively realized that a limit had

been reached. A few statistics bear me out; if we confine ourselves to keyboard sonatas (which for reasons I shall explain later I have decided to do in this book), Haydn wrote approximately sixty, of which some have been lost, Mozart produced about twenty, Beethoven thirty-two, even if we omit some earlier works, Schubert fifteen, Brahms three, Chopin three (of which one is never played), Schumann three plus several abortive efforts, Liszt two, one of which is really a programme piece based on Dante. In the twentieth century, only Prokofiev has added substantially to the repertoire, the sonatas of Skriabine, Rachmaninoff or Hindemith all having failed to survive the hazards of changing fashions. Where once the young composer, striving to establish his right to be taken seriously, would automatically turn his thoughts to the sonata as a suitable form,[1] nowadays the passport to success lies in thinking up a title with vaguely scientific connotations—Polymers II, Octogram, or Extrapolation would all do nicely.

Unlike Gibbons though, I prefer not to concentrate overmuch on the 'Decline and Fall', but rather to focus my attention on the period when the sonata was the predominant form, whether in the guise of orchestral symphonies, quartets or as a solo work. I lay no great claim to scholarship, nor is this intended to be a scholarly or definitive book; but a brief historical survey would seem to be demanded at this point.

The word Sonata itself simply means a 'sounded piece', as opposed to Cantata, 'a sung piece'. In other words, sonatas began life as instrumental compositions of no determined form. The word first crops up with any regularity in the early seventeenth century, and the one relevant factor that is worth mentioning is that these very early examples did have a tendency to consist of several clearly defined sections of music of varying speeds. As the term became more widely accepted, a division between secular and sacred became apparent; the *sonata da chiesa* or church sonata contained music of a consciously lofty tone; the *sonata da camera* or chamber sonata tended to be more dance-like. It would be dangerous to pursue hereditary principles too far, but in the matter

[1] For example, Brahms, Op. I, Alban Berg, Op. I, Prokofiev, Op. I.

of content and intention, I suppose one could say that Beethoven's Op. 31 No. 3, one of his lightweight sonatas, is descended from the *sonata da camera*, while Op. 110 is certainly a *sonata da chiesa*. But as I have already suggested, the evolutionary process moved at such a pace that it is difficult to trace the sort of consistent thread that would appeal to a logical and scientific mind. If we start with Domenico Scarlatti, which for all practical purposes is a reasonably sensible place to begin, the great majority of the compositions which he called Sonata are single movements, very often limited to one rhythmic or melodic idea, pattern music of enormous vitality and inventiveness, but having no relationship to textbook concepts of sonata form. Indeed, they emphasize how important it is to keep a clear distinction between the Sonata, which is a genre, and Sonata Form, which is a plan. However, there are certain of the Scarlatti sonatas which do contain clearly defined contrasts of theme which it would not be too presumptuous to label first and second subjects. C. P. E. Bach, Haydn and Mozart brought the traditional shape of a sonata form movement into being,[1] while at the same time creating a three-movement pattern, normally conceived as a fairly quick and positive first movement, a lyrical and elaborately decorated slow movement, and a finale which could be a dance movement of some kind such as a jig or minuet, or that multi-decker musical sandwich known as a rondo. The essential difference between this new three-movement plan and the long established Suite lay in the size of the movements and the limitation of their number. A suite might well consist of six or seven different dances, Allemande, Courante, Bourrée, Sarabande, Menuet and Gigue; a sonata tended to be limited to three movements, of which only one might be in a recognizable dance rhythm.

Paradoxically, the next step might be argued to be retrogressive, for it involved adding a fourth movement, which would seem to indicate a hankering after the greater variety offered

---

[1] I am not discounting the previous contributions of Wagenseil, Hasse, Kuhnau, Galuppi and others; the idea was in the air for some time, but it took men of C. P. E. Bach and Haydn's stature to give ultimate authority to an emerging concept.

by the suite. Since it was largely Beethoven who was responsible for this innovation, I am inclined to believe that it was
a concession he was prepared to give his audiences in exchange
for first movements of tougher intellectual fibre. As early as
Op. 2, he was producing first movements of considerable length
that demanded concentration of a high order from listener and
player alike—this at a time when most music was still exceedingly
trivial and listened to with little respect. To throw in an extra
dance movement (or scherzo) may well have struck Beethoven as
sound psychology at the least. The four-movement sonata set a
new fashion, but increasingly, the seriousness of purpose established in the first movement began to spread to the other movements as well. Their entertaining function receded into the past;
the slow movement, once a sort of song without words, increasingly became the vehicle for profound, tragic or musico-philo-
sophical thoughts; the scherzo, once a soufflé, was liable to
become a storm, and the finale, so often an exuberant delight in the
hands of Mozart or Haydn, more and more assumed the manner of
an apotheosis. The heroic sonata was born, ironically enough at
the very moment that the form began to disintegrate.

The very word 'heroic' has a whiff of romanticism about
it, and the comparatively rapid decline of the sonata coincides
with the emergence of the Romantic Movement in the second
quarter of the nineteenth century. Beethoven's contribution
to the development of the sonata was two-fold; he enlarged
it and then destroyed it, a statement which I shall elaborate
considerably in a later chapter. Innumerable pages have been
written in the past by writers determined to prove Beethoven's
mastery of the integration of irreconcilable ideas in his late works;
it is as though they were apologizing for his eccentricity in thus
perversely avoiding the road to academic respectability. The
easier explanation seems to have escaped them—that he was not
integrating the irreconcilable, but presiding over the *dis*integration
of the sonata form. (Hence Benjamin Britten's percipient remark,
'It was Beethoven who started the rot . . .') What were the forms
that replaced it? Ballades, Rhapsodies, the Caprice, Intermezzo,

Scherzo (in Chopin's sense) and the unashamedly literary or descriptive piece based on some non-musical inspiration—Night Pieces, Kreisleriana, Fantasy, St. Francis walking on the waters, Apparitions, Legend. In such a climate, the sonata could scarcely be expected to flourish, depending as it did on the calculated balance of phrase against phrase, on the concentrated development of a limited number of ideas, and on a belief in pure musical values. Surrounded as it was by a certain aura, the sonata continued to exist; it was a form to which a composer would pay homage, a guarantee of respectability that was always acceptable to the musical establishment. But with the slow collapse of tonality in music, one of the greatest strengths of sonata form was destroyed; new disciplines took over, and we have now reached a period when few composers are really concerned with a structure that is no longer relevant to the contemporary language, even though in the past, it proved to be the most adaptable and comprehensive form of all time.

If I seem to have arrived at a funeral oration already, it is only because this survey has necessarily been brief. This is not a history book, nor is it an instruction manual on how to write a sonata. It presupposes that a sonata makes more substantial demands on the listener than a descriptive piece, in which the whole receptive process is bound up with images planted in the mind by a title. Call a work Valses Nobles et Sentimentales, Capriccio Espagnole, Nights in the Gardens of Spain, L'après-midi d'un faune or even Ionizations, and you have at least forged a link of sorts with the listener before a note is heard. Debussy's decision to print titles of his Preludes at the end of the piece instead of the beginning was a tacit admission that to use a title, especially one so alluring as La Fille aux cheveux de Lin, was a form of cheating—though it might be argued that he was also underlining their pictorial nature in this way. If you visit an art gallery, you look at the pictures first, and only after the visual impact has made its impression do you stop to read the small plaque that tells you that it is Mrs Veronica Stapleforth or The Harbour at St. Tropez.

A sonata is a very different proposition; although it *can* be descriptive (and many of the early church sonatas were), it is much more likely to be abstract, concerned with purely musical ideas treated in a purely musical way. Much has been written about sonata form, and indeed it is important to have an idea of what it is. My complaint about conventional analysis is that it is so obsessed with anatomy that it takes no account of function. Even the most serious-minded medical student would be unlikely to say to his beloved, 'What a beautiful epidermis you have'. The language of anatomy and the language of love are not the same; nor does it make me love a passage in a Beethoven sonata more to know that a sharpened tonic note is changed enharmonically from D♯ to E♭ thereby becoming the minor third of a C minor triad. Technical jargon gives a feeling of intellectual superiority to its exponent, but it is no guarantee of sensibility.[1] Since inevitably I am going to have to introduce a few technicalities into this chapter, I should like to make my position very clear on this point; if it is not too much of a digression I will turn for a few moments to a symphony, Beethoven's 'Eroica', which, for the purposes of the argument, we may as well call a sonata for orchestra. The passage I am concerned with comes at the end of the development, just before the return of the opening material. I want to examine several different critical reactions to the work.

We need not bother ourselves overmuch with the *Harmonicon*, a musical magazine of the 1830s, which said that if this symphony was not abridged in some way it would soon be totally neglected. Let us turn instead to the literary and poetic type of analysis as exemplified by Sir George Grove.[2]

The tumult of the day has subsided, and all is gradually hushed; the low horns and other wind instruments add to the witching feeling, and a weird twilight seems to pervade the scene. At length the other instruments cease their mysterious sounds, and nothing is heard but the violins in their softest tones, trembling

---

[1] A choice example I came across recently: 'our understanding of the shape of Chopin's E flat Prelude is genuinely widened if we see it not merely as A B A Coda, but as a single amphibrach in which the accent is itself an iambic group'. Is it?

[2] Sir George Grove: *Beethoven and his Nine Symphonies*, Novello, 1896.

as if in sleep, when the distant murmur of the horn floats on the ear like an incoherent fragment of a dream. It is one of those departures from real life which never trouble us in our sleep. But it is enough to break the spell; the whole changes as if by a magic touch, and the general crash restores us to full daylight, to all our faculties, and we find ourselves at home in the original subject and original key.

Now Grove is full of admirable stuff, and I should be less than fair if I suggested that this was entirely characteristic of him. The danger of it lies in suggesting to an unknowing listener that this is what Beethoven was describing in his music—which is pure conjecture, and almost certainly wrong. So what about a different approach, this time from Riezler in his book on Beethoven.[1] He appreciates the harmonic daring of that famous horn entry, as indeed all the commentators do, but he tries to explain it in purely 'musical' terms. This is what he says:

> . . . only here is the third of the scale sounded simultaneously with the fourth, i.e. the seventh of the dominant—and that without any preparation. With some degree of artifice it is perhaps possible to construe the G–E♭ as the second of three parallel thirds of which the first, A♭–F, is given to the second clarinet and third horn, and the third, F–D, to the second clarinet and first bassoon. But apart from the four bars' rest in between, the A♮–F is an octave higher than the horn's G–E♭. We must content ourselves with looking upon the entry of the tonic, while dominant harmony is sounding, as an unusually bold and striking unprepared dissonance.

I, for one, would prefer to know nothing whatever about music than to feel it was really necessary to discuss it in these terms, erudite though they may be. Let us turn at once to Donald Tovey, whose scholarship was impeccable, but who also valued the gift of communication.[2]

---

[1] Walter Riezler: *Beethoven* (trans. G. D. H. Pidcock): M. C. Forrester, 1938.
[2] Donald Francis Tovey: *Essays in Musical Analysis*, Vol. I: Oxford University Press, 1935.

... we are waiting on the threshold of the original key in breathless suspense for the return of the first theme. At last the suspense becomes too much for one of the horns, who, while the echoes of the dominant chord are still whispering, softly gives out the tonic chord of the theme. The orchestra instantly awakens and settles down to recapitulate the opening.

For my taste, that rings truer than any of them, for where Tovey is such a wonderful analyst is that music is like a living thing to him; that phrase about the suspense becoming too much for one of the horns seems to me to capture exactly the humanity of Beethoven's music. From his incredibly comprehensive knowledge of Beethoven, Tovey has formed a very vivid conception of his creative processes; he thinks himself into Beethoven's brain, and the illumination that stems from this is wonderfully revealing. He neither tries to force the music to fit a preconceived theory, nor does he attempt to explain it in literary, psychological, philosophical or pictorial terms.

The words 'sonata form' have already appeared many times in this chapter; the time has come for me to tackle the subject, even though by now one tends to assume that it is something that every listener is familiar with. I have already given in an earlier volume (*Talking about Symphonies*) a fairly detailed analysis which it would be tiresome to duplicate; let me rather suggest a different approach which emphasizes what the musical anatomists are so liable to forget—that form was not invented to satisfy the requirements of music examinations, but is the means whereby the musical drama, in the theatrical sense of the word, is created. You cannot create surprise without having first created a sense of expectation; it is through the use of form that the listener is led to believe something is likely to happen; it is by doing something else that the composer engages our attention, leading us to the paradox that form is most useful as a means of creating 'anti-form', or surprise. Certainly this is not its only function, but it is the one most neglected in the conventional approach to the subject.

Since I have just used the word 'drama', let us imagine a

visit to the theatre where we are to see a one-act play in three scenes. The curtain rises and we see a room in which there are several characters; the conversation may be quite lively, but we get an impression that one individual is more important than the others; there is at any rate a certain feeling of unity about the group. Gradually we have a feeling that someone else is about to arrive; there is a sense of expectancy in the air, we hear a car outside, footsteps on gravel, a door opening and closing. Into the room comes a new character, a girl perhaps, and with her arrival, the whole atmosphere changes. Contact is established, and the scene ends.

Now in musical terms, this Scene One is the equivalent of the so-called Exposition; our opening group of characters is the First Subject (which is much more likely to be a 'group' of ideas than a single melody), the period of expectancy is the Bridge Passage, the entry of the girl with its accompanying change of mood is the Second Subject, and the establishing of contact is a sort of rounding off, sometimes referring to elements of the first subject, and known technically as a Codetta. Let us return to our theatre.

In the second scene, we learn a great deal about the characters that we had not suspected before. The rather quiet clergyman turns out to be a detective in disguise, the girl we had imagined to be the heroine proves to be a blackmailer, and so on. Totally new characters may well be introduced and assume great importance, but this is unusual. In terms of a sonata form movement, this is the Development section; its purpose is to change our ideas of the emotional, rhythmic or melodic characteristics of any of the elements that have been presented to us in the Exposition. Their proportions may be changed, one fragment may be hammered home many times, the order of events may be turned upside down, and new ideas can be introduced, although this is the exception rather than the rule. We should never forget though that the word 'rule' is a dangerous one, for sonatas adhere to principles rather than rules. I shall never forget seeing a young student's copy of the so-called Moonlight sonata in which she had annotated in

minute detail all the proper perquisites of a sonata form movement, First Subject, Bridge Passage, Second Subject, End of
Exposition, Development section and Recapitulation, regardless
of the fact that Beethoven himself described the movement as a
Fantasia and omitted to observe any of the 'rules' of normal
sonata form. Willy-nilly, he had to be forced into the corset
of academic form by the girl's teacher to satisfy her determination
that if it said 'Sonata' at the top of the page, it had got to behave
like a sonata at whatever cost to commonsense. It reminded me of
the classic remark which actually appeared in a printed analysis—
'In this sonata, the second subject comes first . . .' Truly the
academic mind inhabits a world of its own.

Mention of the Recapitulation above brings me to the third
scene of our imaginary play. It begins just as Scene One had
begun, the same group of people, the same sense of expectancy,
even the same arrival of the girl. But because we have now
seen these characters in a different light, because we have got
to know all sorts of things about them that we didn't know
before, they now have a completely new significance for us.
We view their relationships differently; superficially they may
appear to be the same, but the purpose of the drama has been
to uncover their secrets. Reverting to the sonata again, this
is what the Recapitulation is about. It is not a hollow convention,
designed to pad out the music by needless repetition; it is a
reassessment, essential after the surprises and shocks that any
good Development section will have produced. There may well
be further surprises in store, and I cannot stress too often how
much the classical composer uses form as a way of exploiting
surprise. Beethoven in particular is a composer who takes a
schoolboyish delight in inviting you to sit down, and then
whipping the chair away just as you are about to do so.

It is infinitely more important to appreciate the dramatic
implications of sonata form than it is to be able to label every
phrase and chord with some analytical jargon. Form is only
meaningful it it serves some purpose, and by turning to the
theatre for my analogy I have chosen deliberately. There is

one further point that is essential for us to grasp, however, and that is the whole concept of 'key' or 'tonality'. Nobody can have seen a concert programme without seeing the mystic words 'In A Major', 'In C Minor', or whatever it may be. (Denis Matthews once showed me a programme for one of his recitals in which an Afghanistani printer had enthusiastically proclaimed, 'SONOTA IN C MIOR by BEEHOVEN', which really was an instance of mystic words.) To a classical composer, tonality was enormously important. Being an issue that I explored in considerable detail in the first chapter of *Talking about Symphonies*, I shall try to be brief now; but it is an issue that cannot be avoided.

Western music uses seven notes named after the first seven letters of the alphabet, A–G. On each of these notes we can build either a scale, known as the major scale, or two alternative scales known as the minor ('harmonic' minor or 'melodic' minor). The whole complex of notes contained within such a scale, be it major or minor, is what we term 'key'. The keys which are most like, or closely 'related' to use the proper term, are those which have the greatest number of notes in common. Two of these relationships are particularly important. The first one concerns what are called 'relative' major or minor keys. If I play the scale of C major on the piano, it consists entirely of white notes. If I play the scale of A 'melodic' minor, it too consists entirely of white notes. (The 'harmonic' minor has one black note.) A minor is therefore the 'relative' minor of C major, since it shares the same notes, and this relationship is always explained in this way. Needless to say, the reverse holds true; C is the relative major of A minor. If I move into the scales where a number of black notes may be used—A♭ major for instance—I can still find the relative minor by going down to the third semitone below A♭, which would be F, and F minor will therefore share the same notes as A♭ major. The relative minor of any major key is always based on the note three semitones *below* the starting point of the major key, and it shares what is called the key signature, the cluster of sharps or flats that indicates the key at the beginning of each line of the music. There are certain refinements to the system which you will either know if you are musically literate, or which you do not need to know if you don't want to; but this simple diagram should make the pattern clear. The capital letters represent major keys, the small letters represent minor keys. The key signatures are above and below respectively.

Fig. 1

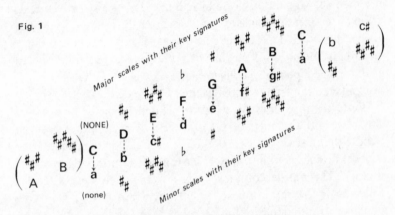

Now, because the scale written in capital letters consists only of white notes, our picture is still incomplete. There are notes like A *flat* (the black note immediately below A), B flat, D flat, E flat and G flat[1] to be taken into account; but the principle would be the same, and since this is not a textbook on the rudiments of music, I shall not belabour the point. What I hope I have conveyed is the fact that a major key and its relative minor are closely 'related', since they have so many notes in common.

I should mention here that though to a layman it sounds as if E major and E minor ought also to be very closely related, to a composer they are markedly different. Our diagram shows why. Look above the capital E and you will see a little cluster of four sharps, the key signature of E major. Look below the small e, and you will see only one sharp, the key signature of E minor. So it is easily understood that E major and C sharp minor, which share the same key signature, are more closely related than E major and E minor which do not. But against this must

[1] These have the alternative names of G♯(A♭), A♯(B♭), C♯(D♭), D♯(E♭), and F♯(G♭).

be weighed the tremendous power, the anchor-like quality of the basic note of any key; a different sort of relationship can therefore be established by playing a phrase first in (say) E major and then in E minor. There is a substantial change, because of the very positive difference in notes; but there is still a quality of '"E"-ishness' about both phrases, a family likeness, though a marked difference of temperament.

Now I said that there were two relationships that were particularly important. We have explored, admittedly rather superficially, the major–minor relationship. The other, and really more significant one, concerns the 'tonic' and 'dominant', terms which crop up in every analysis of a classical sonata, but which again I must attempt to clarify, much as I detest the appearance of a textbook which this chapter is rapidly assuming. The basic, 'home' note of any scale or key, is called the 'tonic'. The fifth note of the scale is called the 'dominant'. On our diagram, if we regard A as the tonic, then E would be the dominant; if C is the tonic, then G would be the dominant. Remembering that the reason for the 'related' quality of two keys was the number of notes they had in common, we find that there is only one note different between a scale started on any note, and the one started a fifth above it. Look at the signature above the D and you will see two sharps. Go up a fifth to A and you will see three sharps; so there is only one more sharp and therefore only one note different.[1] Here then is another fundamental relationship, perhaps the most important of all in classical sonata-form movements. It is virtually the unbroken rule that whenever the First Subject is in a major key, the Second Subject will be in the dominant of that key;[2] furthermore, the Exposition will finish in the dominant.

There is an interesting little side-issue to this. Second Subjects have the reputation of easing the tension, of tending to be more

[1] It is an intriguing fact that as far as key signatures are concerned, moving to the dominant in 'sharp' keys involves adding a sharp, while moving to the dominant in 'flat' keys means taking a flat away. But in effect, to turn a flat into a 'natural' is to raise or sharpen it; therefore, regardless of flat or sharp signature, the dominant key is always one degree 'sharper' than the tonic.

[2] But see pp. 128-129.

lyrical than First Subjects. One perfectly good reason for this is that
all dominant keys are major. The dominant of C major is G major
as we have discovered; but so too is the dominant of C minor,
though it's liable to be a little half-hearted about it. Just as Sonata
Form and a Sonata are not the same thing, there is a difference
between a dominant *key* and a dominant *harmony*. In a composition
in C minor we are often likely to meet this sort of passage.

These are alternations of dominant and tonic harmony, but
it hasn't really established the dominant *key*, since to do that
I should have to change the E flats to E naturals. (Introducing
an F sharp somewhere would also help.) Now, the E♭ is a very
important component of C minor, so important that a composer
is unlikely to sacrifice it willingly. A different convention therefore
emerged in sonatas in minor keys; the Second Subject, instead
of being in the dominant, was put into the relative major, a key that
was much easier to establish. However, this only extends the
proposition I have put forward above; since all dominant keys are
major, we can logically assume that all Second Subjects are in the
major.[1] This is the true family likeness that Second Subjects share,
and it is a much more reliable assumption to make than that they
are all 'feminine' or 'lyrical'.

Much against my nature, I have been driven into the use
of jargon; but though the explanations may have seemed
laborious, the information is essential to the understanding of
the way a composer's mind works when he is writing a sonata.
To sum up, we have seen how a form evolved from simple
beginnings to immense complexity, a complexity that could be
said to have carried the seeds of self-destruction. We have, in
our theatrical analogy, realized the true purpose of form, which,
far from being a straitjacket, is rather a means of creating
'situations'—of surprise, of release, of affirmation or denial.

---

[1] Obviously, there are exceptions, but they are a rarity.

Finally, and I am afraid rather laboriously, we have faced one fundamental truth about the language of Western music, and that is that keys can be closely related, or, conversely, far removed from each other. The key of C, which has no sharps, is very distant from the key of F♯, which has six. Every note of the key of F♯ major, except for one, is an absolute denial of all that is intrinsic to C major. A modulation or shift to such a key is therefore a journey of extreme significance in terms of classical music. Without realizing this, we cannot appreciate many of the most imaginative and daring strokes of the composer. At the risk of being wearisome though, I must repeat that to be able to identify such a modulation, classify it and correctly label it is an empty and meaningless achievement unless one also feels the emotional impact, the lessening or increasing tension, the sense of journeying into remote territory, or the relief of a safe return. Sonata form is the framework for a musical adventure; if the journey is cerebral rather than physical it need be no less absorbing. The ensuing chapters might be said to be route-maps, intended to draw your attention to worthwhile landmarks on the way. I had originally meant to introduce a note of variety by exploring sonatas for two instruments as well as those for piano solo; but the piano literature is so vast that it really demanded a volume to itself. Equally, it would pay scant respect to the wealth of wonderful violin sonatas were I to select two or three and shuffle them into a sort of bargain basement at the end of the book. If I did succeed in choosing three violin sonatas, how should I then eliminate those for cello or clarinet? To coin a phrase, outside each slim volume are a lot of fat chapters wanting to get in; there cannot be room for them all. My choice therefore has been made on one ground and one alone, my deep love of the music which we are now equipped to explore.

CHAPTER II

HAYDN

Sonata in E♭ Major
No. 49 in Collected edition, but also known as Op. 66

Composed 1789–90. Published 1791. Dedicated to Marianne
von Genzinger.

1. Allegro (non troppo). 2. Adagio cantabile. 3. Tempo di
Minuetto [*sic*].

CONSIDERING THEIR NUMBER, the Haydn sonatas are still
curiously neglected. One would expect them to be the
happy hunting ground of any reasonably competent amateur
pianist, yet, surprisingly, only two or three of the fifty or so that
are available seem to have found general acceptance. I have
chosen this sonata rather than the 'big' E Flat[1] precisely because
it is the sort of music that tends to be under-estimated. Even
to identify the piece is something of a problem; as well as being
Op. 66 and No. 49, it is No. 3 in the first volume of the Peters
edition edited by Martienssen, as it is in the Hansen (Parlow)
edition. It also certainly exists in various volumes of selected
sonatas, few of which have any great pretensions to authenticity
with regard to matters of phrasing and the like. An unsympathetic
ear could easily dismiss the opening phrases as trite, over-sym-
metrical, and having a singularly unappealing left hand accompaniment that can sound more like grunts than harmony. (We must
remember the enormous difference in weight of tone between
Haydn's instrument and a modern grand piano.)

[1] Composed 1798; No. 1 in the Peters edition.

Ex.1

The last four notes of the example above show the start of
a phrase that exactly matches the first, except that it is based
on the dominant instead of the tonic. It is easy enough to dismiss this as being altogether too tidy and predictable, but we
must first remember that symmetry was much valued in the
eighteenth century. Haydn spent most of his creative life in
dwellings of the utmost splendour, serving one of the richest
princes in Europe. Wherever he looked, he would have been
aware of the symmetrical balance so favoured by architects
of the time; visual and musical terms even become interchange-
able when we speak of the 'harmonious' perfection of a building,
and it is hardly surprising that Haydn subscribed to the commonly
held belief that a sense of order bred spiritual satisfaction. Part
of his genius lies in his skilful exploitation of symmetry, knowing
the exact moment when to foil our expectation by introducing
something unexpected. The true function of this opening phrase
is to say, 'Here is the key of E flat major; kindly remember it,
as it is important that you should realize when I decide to wander
into other keys'. It is a message which is to be found at the start
of nearly every classical sonata. Time after time, we find that the
opening theme of a work is designed to establish a tonal centre;
to take two of the best known examples (not in sonatas admittedly),
the two hammer blows that begin Beethoven's Eroica symphony,
or the torrent of notes that pour from the soloist's fingers at the
start of the Emperor concerto are both ways of saying exactly
the same thing that Haydn states with such elegance in this sonata.
The chords in the Eroica are abrupt and uncompromising; the
opening cadenza of the Emperor is grandiloquent; Haydn's
opening phrase is beautifully poised, unassuming but gracious.

Having made the point, having established the feel of E flat major beyond doubt, he starts the first journey away from 'home' with a phrase that rises, terrace-like, in easy stages.

Ex. 2

The progression is beautifully sustained, leading us in due course to a complete halt on a chord that is clearly destined to bring us to the dominant key of B flat. The stage is set for the appearance of the second subject, and if Haydn had been the sort of person to accept orthodox procedures without question, he would certainly have introduced his second subject here. (The example begins with the 'halt' chord, which is marked with a pause.)

Ex. 3

Since I composed this myself, I must not be too scathing about it. Suffice it to say that Haydn avoids such an obvious plan, preferring to catch us unawares by suddenly reverting to the opening pattern of the sonata—a move that is roughly equivalent to landing on the head of a snake in 'Snakes and Ladders,' and having to go back and start all over again. One would think that this was surprise enough; but having caught us off our guard, he follows up his advantage with another, more subtle surprise. Ex. 4 shows Haydn's double twist, starting from the same point as Ex. 3.

Ex. 4

The little descending scale in Ex. 4 may seem unimportant
enough; but seen in relation to Ex. 1 it represents a significant
new departure. 'Why, what's this?' Haydn seems to say, and
turning it upside down, promptly finds a use for it. The apparent
irrelevance is transformed into the second subject; the surprise
has been justified.

Ex. 5

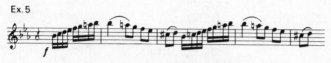

The music chatters along happily enough until our attention
is caught by a near-operatic duet between a very deep bass and a
very high soprano, both parts being played in turn by the right
hand.

Ex. 6

Each 'voice' has the phrase twice, the second version being
the more elaborate. A descending sequence of two-note chords
flits down the keyboard, only to land on a very unexpected
chord indeed.

Ex. 7

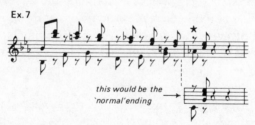

this would be the
'normal' ending

Composition consists partly of moments of discovery; not
everything in a movement is planned from the start, and I strongly
suspect that Haydn was led to the chord marked ★ by chance,
even though such diversions have now been safely catalogued in
harmony textbooks as 'interrupted cadences'. At any rate, the
effect of this interruption is remarkable, a stunned and incredulous
silence as though the composer was thinking to himself, 'What

am I going to do now?' Eight times he repeats the chord, as
though questioning its validity, before he sees a way out of
the impasse and bursts through to the required destination of
B flat major, the dominant key in which the Exposition must
properly end. Here, to save space, are the bare bones.

Ex. 8

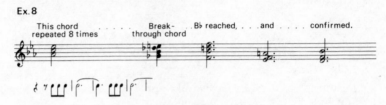

Safely arrived at the goal of B♭, he wraps it up with a throw-
away phrase that seems little more than a convention.

Ex. 9

At this point, the end of the Exposition, the composer would
traditionally draw a thick double line across the music, a 'double-
bar', and expect the performer to play the whole of the music
a second time. It was a way of establishing the importance of the
material, and of fixing both the proportions of the movement and
the order of events in our minds. If a Development section lies
ahead, it is as well that we should have a clear idea of what is likely
to be developed, and repetition enables us to have a better chance of
storing the music in our memories.

Now I have already suggested that this sonata is a very good
example of the sort of music that audiences are all too ready
to take for granted. There is a tendency to sit back, listening
to what might easily be dismissed as tinkling eighteenth-century
piano writing, while secretly we are longing for the time when
the soloist will get on to some meatier stuff—a nice lash-up of
Liszt perhaps. The whole purpose of this chapter is to show how
superficial and misguided such a view is, for once we realize how
cleverly Haydn avoids anything trite or predictable, the sonata is

revealed as a work of genius. The very opening notes of the development are a striking instance of what I mean.

The normal procedure, to judge by far the greater bulk of sonatas of this period, would be to begin the Development with a reference to Ex. 1, though it would be stated in the dominant key, since that key has now been firmly established. In other words, the betting must heavily favour the supposition that the next notes we are going to hear will be these:

Ex.10

The composer might well carry on from here by taking a different turn, but the link with the opening of the sonata will have been established. If by any chance, the composer decides *not* to refer to the opening theme, the next likelihood is that he will choose another idea of established importance, but even this is fairly unusual. I very much doubt though if any listener of Haydn's day, or of any other day for that matter, would have succeeded in guessing what Haydn's decision was to be. Scorning every one of the main themes, he seizes on the most insignificant musical object (subject is altogether too pretentious a word for it); it is Ex. 9, the little tag with which he had rounded off the exposition. This bobtail of a theme is now exposed to the full expertise of a great composer. Time and again he unfolds it, now in the right hand, now in the left, spinning intricate counterpoint with consummate ease.

Ex.11

(a derivation)

Not only is it marvellously unexpected; it also gives us a completely new texture in the music, quite unlike the sound of anything in the exposition. For half a page, he plays tag with this pattern until at last he tires of the game. Only then does he allow Ex. 1 to re-appear; even so, it is in its secondary form (Ex. 4), and for the first time it is in a minor key. The whole natural momentum of the movement has been disturbed by the inspired interruption that Ex. 11 represents, and quite a storm now builds up, angry scales based on Ex. 5 and modulating into all sorts of unexpected directions. You will remember that I said that the real function of Ex. 1 was to say, 'Here is the key of E♭ major'. I think there is considerable support for this view, when we realize that the entire development section only contains one brief reference to Ex. 1, and that in a somewhat disguised form.

At the heart of the movement is a passage of sheer magic; like Ex. 11, it is a brilliant extension of what at first seems a relatively unimportant idea. Haydn suddenly becomes fascinated by the repeated-note pattern shown at the bottom of Ex. 8 (p. 28). Like a conjurer producing objects out of thin air, up here, down there, from his elbow, from his knee, from the back of his neck, Haydn now culls this fragment from different areas of the key-board, never predictable, and yet, because of its rhythmical symmetry, perfectly satisfying.

Ex. 12

In the process of this game, he gets further and further away from home, until he lands up in the key of G♭ major, one which is fairly far removed from the tonic (E♭), since it is based on a note which beyond all others cancels out the 'major' character of E♭. (The chord of E♭ major consists of the notes E♭, G and B♭; to change this to the minor, one simply alters the G to a G♭. If, in the context of a composition basically in E♭ major, one reinforces the

G♭ by building a solid G♭ harmony on top of it, one has struck a pretty destructive blow against the original tonality.) The way Haydn extricates himself from this situation is delightful; with a series of strong off-beat accents, he elbows his way through a thicket of harmony until he reaches a crisis chord.

Ex.13

The music is still in a state of considerable tension; but it is very much on the threshold of C minor, and C minor, if we remember our formula from Chapter I, is the relative minor of E♭ major, our 'home' key. It is a simple matter for Haydn to change the B♮ in the last harmony of the previous example to a B♭, and having done so, the way home is clear. (See the first part of Ex. 14.)

Now a less inspired composer, assuming he had got this far, would probably have been quite content to plunge straight back into the Recapitulation; as Ex. 14 shows, it's a perfectly satisfactory move.

Ex.14

etc. as in
Ex.1

It is precisely at such moments that a composer of genius proves his superiority. Realizing the inherent danger of too much symmetry, Haydn now disrupts the entire rhythmical structure; first he combines the principal elements of Exx. 1 and 12 into the three-beats-in-a-bar pattern that has been observed all the way through the sonata:

Ex.15

The next step is to foreshorten this, compressing it into units of two beats:

Ex.16

then, and this really is a master-stroke, he eliminates the beat entirely, extending the music into a long ribbon of notes that is intended to be played with complete freedom.

Ex.17

Now any music student will be able to label this passage accurately as a *cadenza*; but unless one appreciates its function, one might just as well call it a kidney or an umbrella. By destroying all rhythmic symmetry in this way, Haydn has created a feeling of 'dis'-order; consequently, when he now does embark on his recapitulation, we have a wonderful sense of things falling back into their rightful place. A monarch cannot be restored to the throne unless he has first been deposed, and the skirmish of Ex. 17 serves to give us the greater reassurance that all's right with the world once Ex. 1 takes over again.

The recapitulation is an admirable demonstration of how many subtle and significant changes a composer can make, while appearing to carry on much as before. The 'terrace' phrase (Ex. 2), is considerably extended and modulates through several new keys; all the business of the 'halt' and the misleading return to Ex. 1 is jettisoned; as for the operatic duet, only one phrase from the soprano remains—the bass has apparently gone to try his luck elsewhere. There is a similar interruption to the one in Ex. 7, but it is followed by a delightful example of Haydn's humour when he makes the pianist seem to be afflicted with a nasty rash of wrong notes, as though, like one of my earliest piano teachers, he was playing the piano with gloves on. The entire procedure of Ex. 8 is followed out, and the movement seems all set to finish tidily and neatly with a repeat of Ex. 9. There follows the most beguiling section of all. Technically known as a coda, it gives a touch of humanity to the movement that I find irresible. Like a small boy searching for any excuse to put off the evil moment of going upstairs to bed, Haydn takes Ex. 9 and seems to say, 'You wouldn't mind me playing this just once more, would you?'. He spins it out a little, coming to rest on this chord, which ensures that he has got us hooked. He then tries the 'terrace' phrase in the left hand (for the first time), builds up to quite a climax, breaks off into a silence, and then seems about to settle for a quiet ending. But no. Once again, Ex. 9 begs for another chance, and again—and again—until, having teased us almost beyond bearing, Haydn seems to pull the pianist away from the keyboard by brute force, overshooting the mark by a couple of notes as he does so.

Ex. 18

What an ending to a movement that is packed with invention, despite its seemingly conventional facade.

I have spent a long time analysing this first movement as there is so much to be learned from it; by comparison to the language of Chopin or Liszt, Haydn employs a very limited musical vocabulary; his structures seem at first glance to be conventional to the point of artifice; yet, as I have tried to show, he reveals extraordinary skill in avoiding the obvious, and his use of form is far more often a means of taking us by surprise than allowing us to predict what is going to happen next.

The slow movement is one of the most elaborate that he ever wrote for solo keyboard, a piece that shows an intensely romantic side to his nature that he is seldom credited with. The many embellishments may at first seem no more than pretty gestures; but while they are integral to the style, they cannot conceal the depth of feeling that lies beneath. Passages like this resemble Mozart at his most tragic;

Ex. 19

In terms of the vocabulary of the eighteenth century this is pregnant with emotion—the rarely used key of B♭ minor, the broken phrases full of catches in the breath that are near to tears, the throbbing accompaniment, the constant use of harmonic tension, every bar beginning with a dissonance. As to the middle section of the movement, it is even more remarkable. Too lengthy to quote here, it employs the most extreme resources Haydn could devise, the hands crossed and using the entire span of his keyboard, modulations into 'extreme' keys, and the passionate reiteration of one phrase that he piles ever higher, continually increasing the harmonic tension beneath. The final gesture is a leap of five octaves, from the topmost note of the piano as it was in his day to the very lowest. In performance, I like to play these two consecutive notes with the same hand, so as to emphasize the enormous gulf between them. Something of its effect on a contemporary audience can still be felt if we play first the top and then the bottom note of a modern piano. It seems an awfully long way!

Even more elaborate versions of the opening material follow; but the decorations seem always designed to enhance the expressive qualities of the music. One strange event is worth mentioning; towards the end of the movement there are two sudden loud chords which pianists often find difficult to make convincing.

Ex. 20

Once again I draw attention to the danger of assuming that labelling a musical event necessarily means understanding it. The chord at the beginning of the second bar of this example is certainly an interrupted cadence, since the 'expected' chord is B♭ major, and Haydn denies this expectation by giving us G minor instead. But what interests me is not the event, but its repercussions. Just as the interruption at the end of Ex. 7 caused a long silence, and then an eightfold repetition of the chord—either incredulous, confirming, or a bit of both—so now the interruption causes a strong reaction. It is a reaction that can be interpreted in several ways. The unthinking player just accepts that Haydn asked that the two following chords should be played loud, plays them loud, and leaves it at that. I prefer one of two explanations. Either Haydn is saying to himself, 'I must resist the temptation to digress again, pull myself together, and stay in B♭ until the end,' which means that one plays the chords as a sort of corrective; or—and this

is a rather more fanciful explanation which appeals to me—
the music *itself* is reacting on Haydn's subconscious against the
violence done to its natural inclinations. It is difficult to explain,
but every composer will know what I mean when I say that
music is capable of assuming a certain power of its own, much as
the characters in a novel may develop personal traits that were no
part of the author's original intention. The composer may create
the idea in the first place, but once created, it works back on his
imagination, even to the point of making positive demands.
A cadence is the most rudimentary example of this. If I play this
chord, or commit it to paper, I have created a situation
which demands to be satisfied. It is not I who makes the demand,
but the music itself. I have merely put four circles onto a framework of five lines, and experience has taught me that they are
symbols for a particular sound. If I move the symbols around to
this position, I satisfy the demand. But if this second chord
is the one I begin with, there is no demand; the chord is satisfied
to exist in its own right.

The first chord is a bit like saying, 'I killed the ——', and
breaking off. It is not a group of words that can readily be left
incomplete. 'I killed him' may not be an everyday statement,
but it does not create the same demand of 'what' or 'who' that
the first phrase does.

Now once it is accepted that music has this power to create
its own demands, my interpretation of the two chords in Ex. 20
becomes less fanciful. It is as though the music itself is saying to
Haydn, 'Why did you do that to me? Why did you stop me from
going to the B♭ chord I wanted to reach?' A sceptic will laugh at
this, saying that it was Haydn's decision to interrupt the cadence,
and that he needn't have done it. I grant that the interruption was
the work of the mind, a conscious act on Haydn's part. My contention is that deep in the subconscious, where the creative springs
have their source, there was a reaction which then led to another
conscious decision on Haydn's part whose motive he probably

didn't realize, the decision to have a silence followed by two loud chords. This would mean that the performer should interpret them as protest chords, protests against the violation of a natural law. As if to confirm this view, there is another interrupted cadence nine bars later; it too is followed by a silence, and then a sudden loud chord which shows the way back to B♭ major.

The third movement of the sonata is a Minuet, though of a rather capricious kind. It is full of delightfully personal touches of craftsmanship, small things for the most part, but none the less significant for that, since in their sum they make for quality. There is one intriguing episode in E♭ minor which anticipates almost exactly the famous modulation that has caused audiences such untold joy in Beethoven's Seventh Symphony.

Ex. 21

If we transpose Haydn's music into A minor it will make the similarity easier to realize. Ex. 22 shows Haydn's melodic line in the right hand, and Beethoven's bare bones lying beneath.

Ex. 22

The link can only be one of pure coincidence, but a comparison of the two treatments of a similar harmonic scheme makes a nice study in the changing language of music.

I have stayed with Haydn long enough; let us move on to Mozart, to whose father Haydn once said, 'I declare to you on my honour that I consider your son the greatest composer I have ever heard; he has taste, and possesses the most consummate knowledge of the art of composition'. Something of that art we shall see in the course of the next chapter.

CHAPTER III

MOZART
Sonata in C Minor K.457

Normally coupled with the Fantasia in the same key, K.475, although the sonata was completed on 14 October 1784, while the Fantasia was finished on 20 May of the following year. The two works were published together with Mozart's sanction, and dedicated to his pupil, Therese von Trattner, the second wife of a publisher and printer. It was designated as Op. XI, which must rank as one of the most misleading pieces of information ever committed to print.

1. Allegro. 2. Adagio. 3. Allegro assai, though the first edition gives Molto allegro, agitato.

IT WOULD be less surprising if the gap of five years that separates this sonata from the one we have just been exploring were slanted in the other direction, for the Mozart sonata seems to stand so much nearer to Beethoven in spirit and in its sheer physical demands. For all its many delights, the Haydn must count as essentially a lightweight composition, even when one takes the remarkable slow movement into account. With this sonata by Mozart we move onto a different plane; all three movements show Mozart at the very height of his powers, strong, turbulent, bold, inventive, tender, lyrical, impassioned—not the sort of adjectives that anyone with only a superficial regard for Mozart would readily associate with him. We know from his recital programmes that Beethoven played this work; indeed, as we shall see, the slow movement of Beethoven's Pathétique sonata contains a phrase so close to Mozart that it could well be a direct crib. (Not necessarily culpable in those days; such borrowings were often regarded as a compliment, and Mozart himself took phrases from other composers on several occasions.) 'Beethovenisme d'avant la lettre' was one critical verdict on this sonata, and more than any other Mozart sonata it seems to lead us directly to the world of Beethoven.

The key of C minor is a warning sign; it was a key Mozart reserved for works of special pathos and tragedy, works which reveal the inner despair that the conventions of a society notable for a pose of insincerity forced him to conceal from all save his most intimate friends. For what it says, the first movement is strangely brief, with an ending so suppressed that it is almost as if Mozart had put a hand over his mouth to stop himself from saying too much. Perhaps it was for this reason that he subsequently added as prelude the marvellous 'Fantaisie',[1] a work packed with emotions so powerful and varied that they run the risk of over-shadowing the sonata itself.

On the face of it, two sonatas from the same historical period could scarcely begin more differently than the Haydn E flat that we have just been examining and this severe but passionate work. Yet it is worth saying that from a structural point of view, both sonatas begin with identical opening gambits. The message, 'Here is the key of ...' remains the same, however different the terms in which it is expressed. Where Haydn is elegant and almost casual, Mozart is alternately severe and poignant. But the balance of tonic and dominant harmony—those words again!—remains the same.

Fig. 2

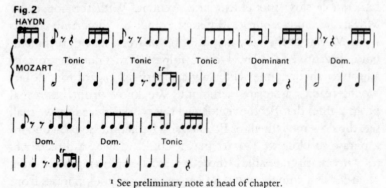

The bone structure is the same, but it is the outer flesh that changes the expression; on Mozart's musical 'face' we see the ravages of despair.

Ex. 23

To be strictly accurate, the chords in bars 4 and 7 are not pure dominant harmony; but by implication, the root of the harmony is dominant, and what has happened is that the chord has been twisted out of true by emotional stress. Smugly to label it a diminished seventh, which is its academic name, takes altogether too isolated a view. Mozart's use of the musical vocabulary is so subtle that he can make a single note sound like a dissonance.

In a bar like this for instance, [musical notation] one 'hears' the chord of E♭ against the first note of the melody, even though he is not so crude as to state it bluntly: [musical notation]

So here, in Ex. 23 bar 4, the *implied* harmony is almost Wagnerian

in its intensity.

Similarly, the true anguish in bars such as those marked with a ⌐‾‾‾‾‾‾¬ can best be shown to our dissonance-hardened ears by taking out the ties; with the resistance offered by the G in the bass, the effect is extraordinary.

Ex. 24

It is easy enough to dismiss these as 'suspensions'; my concern is for the listener to sense and share the pain that caused Mozart to write them.

He continues, keeping the same tension for several more bars; then, stark and unsupported, the opening phrase of Ex. 23 returns, stripped of its darker resonance before being plunged once more into the bass, this time against an angry torrent in the right hand. A new tune appears in the relative major key of E♭; although outwardly calmer, it still betrays an inner agitation as surely as one of Mozart's operatic heroines caught in a compromising situation. At last, her fluttering heart is stilled, and the true second subject appears,[1] as operatic in lay-out as the duet we encountered in Haydn's first movement (see Ex. 6). The human voice was seldom far from Mozart's inner ear, and the essentially vocal nature of this passage is only surprising because of the extremely pianistic style of the rest of the movement.

Ex. 25

---

[1] Because the dominant of a minor key lacks conviction as a true major, the second subject of a movement in a minor key is normally in the relative major. See Chapter I.

The phrasing is revealing here, with the last two notes in bars 1 and 5 specifically *not* marked with a slur; our 'soprano' is still a little disturbed, while the 'baritone' is all smoothness. Just as it seems that Mozart has forgotten all care in the excitement of writing an imaginary operatic ensemble, there is a violent interruption. Thunderous triplets in F minor tax the resources of Mozart's fortepiano to the limit. The former agitation returns, intensified by another vocal trick, short three-note phrases that seem to gasp for air.

Ex. 26

This agitation is sustained right to the end of the exposition, in whose final bars we find something that is interesting for two reasons. The opening phrase of Ex. 23 is made to overlap itself:

Ex. 27

but if we forget about shapes for a moment, and think about performance, we find a subtle detail that shows how punctilious Mozart could be. In the second bar of Ex. 27, it is unthinkable that the rising octaves in the left hand should suddenly be emasculated on the last beat; yet Mozart has written *p*. That this only refers to the right hand is confirmed a couple of bars later, when he gives a further indication of *p* in the left hand. With the much wider range of tone we have become accustomed to on a modern piano, these directions are difficult to observe convincingly; but at least we should be able to accept that Mozart could contemplate the simultaneous projection of two contrary emotions, the strong, heroic octaves, and their frail antithesis. Such a conflict truly bears the hallmark of romanticism.

The development is short and concentrated, preoccupied almost entirely with one idea. The transposition of the opening phrase into the major, as shown at the end of Ex. 27, might suggest a more optimistic turn of events. But this is no true C major, however bravely it may set out. In a flash, Mozart reveals an alternative interpretation of the notes, treating them rather as the dominant of F minor, into whose turbulence he now plunges. We hear just a passing snatch of the theme that had preceded the second subject, and then the storm breaks. Six times, the strong opening phrase beats its way through raging triplet figuration,[1] until at last it cracks. The last two notes break away, and drift down into the abyss.

Ex. 28

In performance, it is essential to isolate the pairs of notes in bars 3 and 4 from the following chords in the left hand. Nothing is more likely to diminish the dramatic pathos of this inspired moment than to hear suggestions of a gavotte.

Ex. 29

Mozart's phrase is no dance; it is the disintegration of a noble idea, the classic hero come to grief, and nobody who understands what is happening can fail to be moved.

At the start of the recapitulation which follows the pause at the end of Ex. 28, we would do well to remember a profound truth about sonata form that is seldom mentioned. Though the notes we now hear are identical with the opening phrase (Ex. 23), our frame of mind is very different. Our emotions have been mightily played upon; we have been purged, and finally cast down. Therefore when we hear these notes again, they acquire a new heroism, the girding-up of the loins after defeat, the deter-

[1] Also, see Ex. 116.

mination to prevail. Properly presented, there should be no sense of *déjà vu* (or *déjà entendu*), for we are hearing this phrase as we have never heard it before.

Like all great composers, Mozart still has a fair number of new developments in store for us in his recapitulation. He finds a more complex way of interlocking the first phrase than the one revealed in Ex. 27, and then introduces a completely new theme, one of the most perfect moments of the entire movement, for in such a context we hardly expect to find anything so tender.

Ex. 30

But, as that last chord shows, we are not let off the rack for long, and when the second subject reappears, it is in the minor, with all the emotional change that that implies. The music continues on its tormented way, though again, moments of tenderness are interpolated in unexpected places. The greatest surprise is still to come, the coda, in which, after the most forbiddingly austere presentation of the opening phrase of Ex. 23, Mozart ends with a striking demonstration of his genius. He takes what in ordinary hands would be a cliché:

Ex. 31

conventional enough, but Mozart puts a *forte* on the fourth beat of bars 1, 2, 4 and 5, and on those beats alone. It gives an extraordinary limping effect; the movement sinks to its death like a wounded animal, and, with a last gasp, peters out into silence. In theatrical terms, it is one of the most dramatic 'curtains' Mozart ever devised.

As with the Haydn sonata of the preceding chapter, we now
find an immensely long slow movement, covering the widest
range of emotion. Not surprisingly it is in the relative major key
of E♭; one of the most valuable things about classical key
relationships is their long-term effect. In the exposition of the
first movement, the only moments of release from tension were
when the music moved into E♭, though the emotional force of the
movement was such that these passages were seldom left undis-
turbed for long. Nevertheless, they did hold out the prospect of
happier things; when, therefore, the second movement allows us
positively to luxuriate in E♭ major, it is as though we have finally
reached the promised land.

Ex.32
Adagio

sotto voce

Again Mozart's instructions are revealing—the rarely used
sotto voce (literally 'beneath the voice', or as one might say, 'in
hushed tones'), the *f* in bar 2 which is totally free from aggression,
but rather has the nobility of horns. The *p* in the second half of
bar 2 warns us against taking the first three notes too loud, and
emphasizes the delicacy of the embroidery.

In the eighth bar a new theme appears, and again one is struck
by the operatic nature of the writing. We could be in the
Countess's boudoir in the second act of Figaro and indeed, there
are remarkably close parallels between this movement and
Porgi amor; differences of notation need not blind us to such
similarities of expression.

Ex.33

FIGARO: ACT II., Opening Aria

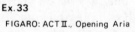

Porgi a-mor, qualche ri - sto-ro al mio duo-lo, a'miei so - spir!

SONATA: K.457. II bars 8-9

FIGARO: idem.

la - - - scia al - men mo - rir

SONATA: bars 11-12

FIGARO: idem. (orchestral part)

8va bassa

SONATA: bar 14

The moral to be learned from these resemblances is that the pianist in such a movement must always strive to achieve the expressive nuance of a singer; however elaborate the embellishments may be, they are essentially vocal in character. On the rare occasions when Mozart's thought becomes entirely pianistic, the style of writing makes the change abundantly clear. There are some notable instances of extreme heroic gestures, sweeping scales that certainly could not be sung.

Ex. 34

Yet even this could be achieved in operatic terms. Are not the scales themselves a way of conveying the sort of dominance we might expect from a heroine, eyes ablaze, her arm extended in peremptory command?

Ex.35

But if it is constructive to compare this movement with Mozart's operatic style, it is equally intriguing to examine the link I have already mentioned between it and Beethoven's Pathétique sonata. The central section of the movement, (bars 24–41), is built upon a new theme of great tenderness and nobility. The key is initially Ab major, but later, after the dramas of Ex. 34, Mozart moves into the more remote world of Gb major, giving the theme a new colour. It is the first version however that seems to have planted itself in Beethoven's mind.

Ex.36

*(Notice the subtle imitation of the melody suggested
by the arrowed notes in the L.H.)*

Now this is a work of Mozart's maturity, while the Pathétique
was composed when Beethoven was about twenty-eight—the
exact date is not certain. A note by note comparison of the two
slow movements would need an inordinate number of music
examples in a chapter of this nature, when both works are so
easily obtainable. It is a study worth making though, there
being no doubt that Mozart emerges as much the more powerful
figure. The Pathétique slow movement is a 'song without words'
of extraordinary beauty; admittedly it has tragic overtones,
and one central climax that generates considerable tension.
Starting from essentially the same melodic root, albeit in the
twenty-fourth bar of the movement, Mozart covers a far wider
range of emotion, gives us much more variety of figuration,
modulates with greater freedom, and stretches the whole
resources of the language of his time to a degree that makes
us realize what a wealth of passion lurks behind this elegant
Baroque facade. A movement that had started in serene beauty
erupts into drama, and it is partly because of the considerable
loss of tonal stability during the central section that Mozart
feels the need to take quite a time in re-establishing a feeling of
security at the end. The last few bars are like a lingering farewell;
one senses a feeling of nostalgia, almost, as Mozart echoes Othello's
forlorn cry,

> O now for ever
> Farewell the tranquil mind, farewell content.

The validity of this possibly over-romantic view is confirmed
by the entire third movement which is almost neurotic in its

intensity. There is scarcely a phrase which does not hint at a soul in torment. Mozart at this stage still kept his troubles largely to himself; the success of the operas sustained him, though he was very much aware of the fickleness of public taste. The creative daemon can be a cruel master though, consuming those on whom it battens. He must have known he was burning himself out, and in September 1784, the month before he wrote this sonata, he became seriously ill with rheumatic fever. For four successive days he suffered fearful attacks of colic with violent vomiting. (In the course of another illness, he was blind for nine days, a traumatic experience.) His was a frail body, and the incessant demands he made on it, composing, playing, travelling, must have taken a heavy toll.

Although the final movement begins quietly there are two clear indications of emotional tension—syncopation and dissonance.

Ex.37

The phrase is repeated an octave lower with a new twist to melody and harmony alike; then the control snaps, and the music breaks into an angry protest.

Ex.38

The 'spread' chords in the right hand give an impression of being ripped from the keyboard at this speed, while the octave

★ But see note concerning the tempo of this movement on p. 39.

leaps in the bass are far from characteristic. It is about as near to an open expression of rage as Mozart ever allows himself to go, except where he has a text in justification, a Dies Irae perhaps or an operatic quarrel. There is a silence that a courageous performer can hold for an incredibly long time, and then a forlorn little phrase of the utmost pathos. Was the sheer impotence of man against the blows of fate ever more cogently or economically expressed? Again Ex. 38 bursts out in anger, again there is the silence, again the unwilling surrender. There follows a single chord, designed at any rate to drag us out of despair into the more tolerable world of E♭ major. But even with the emergence of a new and more lyrical theme the relief is of short duration; it soon becomes distorted by chromaticisms that erode any confidence we might have gained about staying in a major key.

Ex.39

accpt. 8ᵛᵃ bassa   loco

Every attempt to lessen the tension is frustrated; phrases are chopped into fragments, intervals distorted, quiet passages are violently interrupted by sudden accents, the music covers the entire range of the keyboard. Yet, despite the explosive force of the movement (and explosive is the word used by no less an authority than Einstein), Mozart's instinctive command of classical proportions manages to contain the essentially romantic qualities of the music. The movement is perfectly open to analysis as a textbook example of Rondo form.

Bars 1–45   Principal subject in ternary form.
Bars 46–102   Episode in a related key, though if we are to regard the movement as *Sonata* Rondo-form, bars 46–58 would presumably be the Second Subject, and bars 59–102 the Episode.
Bars 103–141 Repetition of principal subject.
Bars 142–145 Mozart being difficult.

Bars 146–166   New Episode in subdominant, followed by repetition in dominant minor.

Bars 167–220   Transposed version of first Episode, now in tonic minor.

Bars 221–231   Repetition of principal subject.

Bars 232–248   Mozart failing his diploma.

Bars 249–274   Repetition of second and third parts of principal subject.

Bars 275–286   Repetition of part of material of second Episode.

Bars 287–end   Final coda.

I concede that if one cannot think of anything better to do with a piece of music, this is a way of passing the time, although what it has to do with *understanding* is past my comprehension. One could construct a composition of absolutely no value that would fit the same ground-plan to perfection; but would that prove that Mozart's music was valueless? Of course not. Therefore the ground-plan in itself is meaningless unless one understands its function as well.

It is a cage within whose confines Mozart has contained fiery and rebellious ideas; it is a strong cage, reinforced by tradition. Mozart's classical self accepts the cage, admitting its usefulness as a discipline; but his romantic self beats against the bars, crying out to be let free. It was that romantic self that felt the need to write a Fantasia as a prologue to this sonata, a prologue which might be interpreted as an assertion of freedom. Had he managed to escape completely from the bonds of convention, he would have ended *Don Giovanni* with the main protagonist's descent into Hell;[1] as it was, Mozart made a concession to the taste of the time, a taste which, to a certain degree, he was willing to respect, for he acknowledged the classical virtues of order and restraint. It is in a sonata such as this that we can see intimations of the direction Mozart might have taken had he lived another ten years. He died, leaving Prometheus still in chains. It was Beethoven who was to assume the role of Hercules in breaking them apart.

[1] As Verdi or Berlioz would certainly have done.

CHAPTER IV

AN INTRODUCTION TO BEETHOVEN'S PIANO SONATAS

THE THIRTY-TWO piano sonatas of Beethoven are his most significant biography, worth more than all the thousands of pages that have been written about him. In them we see not the events of life outside, as we do in most biographies, but the infinitely more important life within. In the sonatas, written clearly for us all to hear, lie the stages of a great composer's development from youth to maturity, a journey which paradoxically began with the complete confidence of a young man, knowing he had the stuff of genius within, and ended in loneliness, cut off from the world by a barrier of silence, pushing bravely but sometimes gropingly into a new era. Beethoven has been described as a cautious revolutionary, but there is certainly no doubt that he changed the entire course of music. The first and last sonatas seem to belong to different worlds, and I doubt if any other composer in history, apart from Stravinsky, so transformed his own musical language.

Hindsight can be dangerous when it comes to interpretative decisions. The very name of Beethoven is surrounded by such an aura that it is easy for us to read too much into the early works, forcing us to fit them to our preconception of what Beethoven ought to sound like in the light of what we know his ultimate achievement to have been. But used discerningly, hindsight can also be very revealing, and the main purpose of this chapter is to trace links that show how Beethoven was continually enlarging his resources rather than radically changing them. Though his nature may have become more surly as the embittering effect of deafness made itself felt, he still remained the same man. The optimistic hopes of the brilliant youth may have become clouded by disease and poverty; but just as we can detect the style of a painter like Van Gogh from his early imitative studies to his last strange masterpieces, so we can find fascinating intimations of mature Beethoven in some of the most taken-for-granted pages of his youth.

Much as an archaeologist uncovers the various layers that conceal a number of civilizations, so now I want to penetrate Beethoven's subconscious so deeply that we find the very sources of his invention; such an exploration must start at the end, at the top layer so to speak; let us begin then with a phrase which shows Beethoven at the summit of his powers in the longest and most complex of all the sonatas, Op. 106, the Hammerklavier.[1] It begins with a gesture of tremendous force.

Ex.40

The most notable features here are the catapult-like spring of the very first two notes in the left hand, the strength of the rhythm, the silences between the phrases, and lastly, the pairing off of the final two chords of each phrase. In best Sherlock Holmes mood, let me concentrate, my dear Watson, on these last two chords. If I lengthen the first chord in bars 2 and 4, I get this.

Ex.41

Turn back more than twenty years to 1796, and we find Beethoven beginning his sonata in E♭, Op. 7, with this theme.

---

[1] Despite its rather emotive sound, the word Hammerklavier simply means 'piano'.

Ex.42

Exciting though this is as a sonata, it is still a very formal piece, with the influence of Haydn in particular clearly to be seen. The left hand here is an unadventurous formula, the chords sit down contentedly enough on the first beats, and in common with most young composers, Beethoven likes to keep the music moving along in case we should lose interest.

Let us now turn to Op. 22, which is not only in the same key as the Hammerklavier, but has several other remarkable similarities as we shall discover. Beethoven has already hit on a much more arresting opening rhythm.

Ex.43

If we make a comparatively small alteration to that, changing the little four-note group  to a three-note pattern slanted in the opposite direction, we arrive at this:

Ex.44

Repeat the first note a couple more times, and even Dr Watson at his most imperceptive could see that this is not all that far removed from the opening phrases of the Hammerklavier.

Without bending the evidence too far then, it can be established that these three sonatas, Opp. 7, 22 and 106, are all saying the same thing in their opening bars, even though the musical vocabulary shows substantially more complexity as Beethoven progresses. In Op. 7, the language is essentially conventional and derivative; Op. 22 shows him finding his way to a much greater individuality of expression—the gaps between the phrases, the alert, vital quality of the rhythm, the restraint implied by the instruction *p*, giving an especially arresting character to what might otherwise be a slightly trivial idea. But both these early sonatas are the music of mortals; in the Hammerklavier he is like a god armed with supernatural weapons, and he commands our attention with the authority of a god.

It would be stupid to discount the importance of the actual development of the piano in the evolution of Beethoven's mature style. We still find it hard to accept that the instrument he used as a young man (when it seems that he was a prodigious player) was not far removed from a harpsichord in sheer weight of sound, having about a quarter of the tonal resources of a modern concert grand.[1] Even if as a young composer his vision had contemplated anything so immense in stature as Op. 106, he would never have committed the notes to paper, since they would have merely sounded ineffective and puny on the only pianos that were available. It is a mistake to assume that the sheer size of a work is somehow related to the age of the composer; the stature of Beethoven's earlier sonatas was very much dictated by the limitations of his keyboard. Brahms, as a young man, had the instruments he needed, and his only three piano sonatas, Opp. 1, 2 and 5, are all conceived on a gigantic scale.

Let us return to the Hammerklavier, picking up with the very next phrase.

[1] For a more detailed discussion of this, see Chapter One of *Talking about Concertos*.

Ex.45

It makes a smooth contrast to the smash-and-grab effect of
the opening bars (Ex. 40); it is clearly melodic, yet not in the
least vocal in conception, as the themes that we found in the
Haydn or Mozart sonatas were. Yet again, we can find a very
similar texture in Op. 22, only a fleeting similarity perhaps,
but worth mentioning.

Ex.46

The two textures are almost identical, but the thought in the
later sonata is so much more varied, and the danger of a mechanical
sequence of textbook modulations is avoided.

Now one of the most striking passages in Op. 22 is the second
subject, a martial phrase totally lacking in those feminine attributes
which are normally regarded as the essential quality of Second
Subjects.

Ex.47

The unusual thing about this is the consistent use of thirds[1]
in both hands; it is a texture you would never find in the keyboard
music of Haydn or Mozart. Turn to the Hammerklavier and we

[1] A third is a two-note chord (or an interval) whose notes are three semitones apart
(minor third) or four semitones apart (major third).

find another instance of the same technique; but where in Op. 22, the two hands march together in parallel, in the later work they go their separate ways, thus adding considerably to the musical interest.

Ex. 48

Beethoven's mature technique no longer allows him to employ the slightly over-simple version of Op. 22; but equally, that simplicity was strong enough for 1799, when it was written.

If this chapter seems to be over-concerned with 'coming events casting their shadow before', it is because the differences between late and early Beethoven are so self-evident that it is a more instructive exercise to pursue the similarities. The enormous changes that he brought about in matters of form have tended to blind us to the remarkable continuity of his language. Certainly it too changed substantially, but whereas his approach to sonata form was ultimately to be destructive (since it ceased to serve any useful purpose), his treatment of what might be termed the basic language of music was to enrich and to extend, but never to destroy. We find similar accompanying figures in works that are twenty years apart; his careful plotting of surprise, his capriciousness of invention, his bluntness, and his ability to think in large paragraphs are constant factors that did not change. Let us pursue the matter a little further.

The exposition of the Hammerklavier ends with three giant steps, struck with all the power the soloist can command.

Ex. 49

Those last two phrases are like dim recollections of the opening theme (Ex. 40), which indeed Beethoven has now left so far behind that we are in danger of forgetting it. They call us back to it like off-stage trumpets, and despite the huge span of the movement the classic convention of repeating the exposition needs to be observed. All the same, one can scarcely imagine a more arresting way of giving the utmost drama to a long-established custom. What does he do the second time round?

Ex.50

Here there is a double surprise; first, the striking change from B flat to B natural on the third note; second, the totally unexpected duplication of the three hammer-like blows at a point when we have been conditioned to expect a distant horn-call.

Some eighteen years earlier, Beethoven had written a sonata in D major (Op. 10 No. 3) whose first subject ends with an identical pattern.

Ex.51

There is no doubt that the three rising notes are meant to be every bit as emphatic, nor that their purpose is to catch our attention. But in the earlier sonata, the gesture is largely wasted, leading as it does to a pleasant enough tune whose texture is virtually identical to a multitude of passages in Mozart or Haydn. The exploitation of surprise in the later sonata is typical of Beethoven's maturity; the same three steps now lead us to mystery and suspense.

A comparison of slow movements can be equally revealing. In Op. 22, which really does seem to have been a direct ancestor

of several of the later works, we find Beethoven beginning in a
fairly conventional mood.

The world of Mozart is not very far away; the accompaniment
is a convention of the time, used almost as frequently as the
more flexible version Mozart preferred . The tune is
elaborately decorated, and even the wide leaps that appear later are
frequently found in Mozart's vocal writing. The harmony to
begin with is the soul of orthodoxy, although there are admittedly
moments in this movement when Beethoven produces chords
that anticipate Debussy.

Ex.53
Op.22.II

Yet astonishing though these harmonies are, they are 'explained'
by their resolution (the subsequent chord), and they are still
enclosed within an essentially eighteenth-century fabric. If then
we deduce a formula from this music, we can say that it consists of
repeated chords in the left hand and a decorated melody in the
right. Even as late as Op.110, Beethoven still clung to this somewhat pedestrian formula. The difference lies in the expressive power
with which he uses it. In the entire piano literature there can be few
passages as profound in their expression of grief as this, and yet the
'formula' is identical.

Ex.54

(Adagio, ma non troppo)

Op.110
III

What an infinitely more individual voice speaks to us here. The slight artificiality of utterance is thrown off entirely; instead, we find an expression so intimate and personal that I feel myself an intruder into Beethoven's privacy when I play it.

The pace of change in our own century has been frightening; there are many people still about who were born before man had learned to fly an aeroplane; in the span of a single lifetime, we have progressed from the first clumsy attempts of the Wright brothers to the Apollo missions to the moon. But the nineteenth century was not exactly stagnant. Had Liszt been born two years earlier he would have been a living link between Haydn and Stravinsky[1]—a gulf that seems like centuries. It was Beethoven more than anybody else who brought about a complete change of view as to what music was capable of expressing. The truly 'classical' composer serves music as something greater than himself, much as a priest serves his God; the 'romantic' composer uses music as a form of self-projection, a public expression of personal emotion. Across the span of the thirty-two piano sonatas, we can observe this change of attitude taking place, and it seems likely that Beethoven's deafness may well have accelerated the process. By being driven ever further into himself, deprived of social contact, it was inevitable that he should increasingly regard music as a means of *self*-expression as opposed to mere expression. In doing so, he opened the door to the Romantic Movement; inheriting the mantle of Haydn and Mozart, he not only reworked the fabric, but changed its entire function. The slow movement of Op. 106 contains clear anticipations of the language of Chopin and Brahms, just as surely as the early sonatas are sometimes unashamedly derivative from Beethoven's great predecessors. In a book of this

[1] Haydn died 1809: Liszt 1811-86: Stravinsky 1882-1971.

size, I cannot discuss more than a very few of the sonatas, but I hope that this introduction has done something to demolish the 'Three-period' theory which has had altogether too long a run. It is the sort of neat, cataloguing approach that appeals to tidy minds—first period, up to 1800 when he was still showing some in-debtedness to the past, second period, 1800–15 during which he began to forge a much more personal style, and lastly, the period from 1815 up to his death in 1827 when he moved out into a world of his own. There is some truth in the theory, but like most such generalizations it can lead to misleading conclusions. I prefer the view I have attempted to convey in this brief introduction, a view that shows the course of Beet-hoven's creative life as an inevitable, almost pre-destined journey. It was a search for a language, the right language to express thoughts and emotions that were certainly dormant in him from his middle twenties. The links I have traced between early and late works may reveal differences of technique; but they also show a similarity of purpose. A man may set his heart on Everest while he is still tackling his first few rock-climbs. Beet-hoven first planned to set Schiller's 'Ode to Joy' to music when he was in his early twenties; it took him the experience of writing eight symphonies to discover how to do it to his satisfaction. Whereas Mozart and Haydn, Bach and Handel were able to write with astonishing fluency because the techniques they had learned were entirely suited to their needs, Beethoven found composition a constant struggle. His sketch-books reveal agonies of indecision; how *could* he express such new concepts of music with a language inherited from his forbears? As a young man, Beethoven did not lack technique; he had all the facility one could wish for. But it was a technique that was no use for climbing his particular mountain. The sketch-books are the clearest evidence of his dissatisfaction with an existing language, of his arduous search for something more adequate. The view of his ultimate destination was inevitably obscure, but the journey began sooner than people realize.[1]

[1] For the full understanding of the following chapters I would recommend keeping a copy of the Beethoven sonatas to hand, the least cumbersome being the *Lea Pocket Scores* (P.O. Box 138, New York 32).

CHAPTER V

BEETHOVEN

Sonata in E♭ Major Op. 31 No. 3

Composed in 1802. Unusually, there is no dedication. Op. 31 Nos. 1 and 2 were first published in 1803 in an edition called *Répertoire des clavecinistes*. A subsequent edition corrected by Beethoven then appeared, still as *Deux sonates, Op. 31, Édition très correcte*. This was published by Simrock, simultaneously with an edition from Cappi of Vienna, still giving only the first two sonatas, but labelling them Op. 29. This sonata first appeared on its own without an opus number, Edition Nägeli, in 1804. In 1805, Cappi brought out all three sonatas in one volume, though they were still erroneously called Op. 29.

1. Allegro. 2. SCHERZO: Allegretto vivace. 3. MENUETTO: Moderato e grazioso. 4. Presto con fuoco.

THE IMAGE OF Beethoven as a frowning giant wrestling with intractable material is so commonly held that I thought it essential to include at least one sonata that would show him in a good humour. There is a wider choice than one would at first imagine. Rather surprisingly, the really dramatic sonatas are in the minority; individual movements may stand out, but the only sonatas I would classify as essentially 'tigerish' would be Nos. 5, 8, 17, 21, 23, 29 and, *hors de concours*, the first movement of 32. Their impact is such that we tend to forget how often Beethoven shows quite a genial face to the world. I think the reason for this lies partly in his complete avoidance of sentimentality; slow movements may be lyrical, deeply felt, poetic or tragic, but they are never saccharine. He knows exactly when to tauten the harmony by a touch of dissonance, or to dispel with a sudden shock any tendency to drift into a vague reverie.

I have sometimes called this sonata 'The Case of the Missing First Subject'. It is a facetious title, but it serves to draw attention to one of the most characteristic aspects of the sonata, its avoidance of the obvious. Time and again, Beethoven lures us into carefully prepared traps, only to show a schoolboyish glee at having fooled us once more. When one remembers that 1802 was the year of the famous *Heiligenstadt Testament*,[1] it is almost impossible to imagine how a man could drag himself out of such a pit of despair to write music that radiates humour from every page. Perhaps Ries gives us a clue when, describing the onset of Beethoven's deafness, he says, 'When occasionally he seemed to be merry it was generally to the extreme of boisterousness; but this happened seldom'. Beethoven was near to suicide; to quote part of the *Testament*:

> . . . but little more and I would have put an end to my life—
> only art it was that withheld me, ah it seemed impossible to
> leave the world until I had produced all that I felt called upon to
> produce, and so I endured this wretched existence—truly
> wretched, an excitable body which a sudden change can throw
> from the best into the worst state—Patience—it is said I must
> now choose for my guide, I have done so, I hope my determi-
> nation will remain firm to endure it . . . [etc.]

The near incoherence of the prose is striking confirmation of Beethoven's extremity of despair. It is at such times that the creative artist is most likely to turn to work for consolation. Human companionship could give him little solace; it only served to remind him of the rapidly encroaching deafness that was to isolate him from society. Op. 31 no. 2, the so-called Tempest sonata, is the music that most accurately reflects the agony of mind revealed in the *Testament*. This third sonata of the set is a marvellous demonstration of the resilience of the human spirit.

The sonata begins with an enigmatic harmony that could be in one of several keys. I have already underlined the impor- tance of tonality in the whole concept of sonata form. Of the

---

[1] A historic document in which Beethoven expressed his despair at growing deaf and losing contact with humanity.

thirty-two piano sonatas, twenty-nine begin with themes that define the home key unmistakably within the first two or three bars. The first sonata to be even a mite ambiguous is No. 15, the Pastoral in D, whose first three bars are a trap, designed to make us imagine that the piece is in G—something like this perhaps:

Ex.55

but as soon as a C♯ appears in the fifth bar, Beethoven shows us that he has been bluffing; the mild ambiguity is a refreshing change from the normal clear definition of a tonal centre.

Now, three sonatas later, Beethoven makes much more conscious play with the idea of keeping us guessing. The opening harmony of the sonata is in no key at all. The Germans call this work *Die Frage*, or 'the Question', and the first notes certainly have an interrogatory flavour.

Ex.56

Even the repetition of the phrase suggests an air of disbelief, as though Beethoven had found his hands playing the chord by chance and then asked himself if he really meant it. When I stated that this was in no key at all, it might seem a rather lunatic assertion; but the fact is that this is the sort of transitional harmony that could lead in several directions. For instance,

Ex.57

which would lead us into quite a serious movement in C minor.
On the other hand we could treat the first bar as the beginning of
a sequence, almost playful in nature, leading to something lyrical
and charming.

Ex.58

This gives us the possibility of a gentle, undemanding sonata in
B♭ major.

Beethoven, having proffered an enigma, soon clarifies it,
removing all doubts as to the tonality of the piece. Indubitably
and emphatically, the fourth bar of Ex. 59 establishes the key
of E♭ major.

Ex.59

Having sat down so firmly in the fourth bar of Ex. 59 (actually
bar 6 of the sonata), there is something very beguiling about the
way the following bar seems to say, 'Now we can relax; we know
where we are'. We have had a brief introduction; our location

has been established; now, surely, we have every right to expect a nice, clearly identifiable First Subject.

Ex.60

A splendid solution of impeccable orthodoxy—which is presumably why Beethoven rejected it. Instead, he goes wandering off into a vague little ascending scale, has another couple of bites at Ex. 56 (one of them with 'this week's deliberate mistake' inserted), states Ex. 59 even more firmly, and once again settles down with a sigh of relief onto the tonic chord of E♭. It's like the sort of scene one might find in *Alice in Wonderland*, a scene in which the heroine finds a mysterious little door (bar 1), taps on it gently (bar 2), laboriously pushes it open (bars 3–6) and goes through into a little courtyard marked E flat (bar 7). She climbs a staircase out of the courtyard (bars 8–9) and at the top of the stairs finds a mysterious little door (bar 10), taps on it (bar 11), pushes it open (bars 12–15) only to find herself in another identical courtyard marked E flat (bar 16). Needless to say, I am not suggesting for one moment that Beethoven is actually describing any such events; but there is a parallel in the way he 'discovers' E♭ major twice, and each time by the same rather curious route.

The well-informed listener sits back, confident that now, at least, a recognizable First Subject will emerge. What happens? Some casual flicks of a duster across the keyboard, mere snippets of phrases—related it is true to Ex. 56, but scarcely having enough substance to be regarded as a theme at all.

Ex.61

If this sonata can be said to have a first subject in the textbook sense of the word, that is it, in its entirety. Everything that precedes Ex. 61 is unquestionably an introduction, and what now follows is equally clearly a Bridge Passage. I defy even Perry Mason to detect so much as another bar of first subject, hence my facetious title.

The bridge passage behaves with complete predictability. It *sounds* like a bridge passage, chattering on like a professor giving a breathless definition of the difference between a scale and a broken chord.

Ex.62

Bridge passages are destined to take us from the tonic to the dominant, and this one does so in exemplary fashion. At last, we feel we have something we can hang on to, something that seems to be behaving as it should. It is precisely at such moments that Beethoven is most likely to catch us off our guard. At the very instant we are confident that the second subject is going to emerge, he plunges us back to square one. No wonder there is an air of depression about the place.

Ex.63

Now this sort of thing is really upsetting; here is Beethoven, apparently getting all soulful ('not a dry eye in the house' by the end of the phrase), and then suddenly, thump, bang, crash, thud, four nasty shocks, each specifically marked with an individual *f* in case the pianist should attempt to soften the blow.

If one is sufficiently determined to force Beethoven into his popular role of Titan, it is possible to take all this quite seriously, to shed tears during the middle of Ex. 63 and then interpret those four rude blows as a cry of protest against destiny or something equally inspiring. That I reject such an interpretation is not due to any inherent frivolity on my part, but to my firm conviction that all the evidence goes against it. So surprising a gesture cannot be taken out of context; we have seen what happened before; the more important question is what happens after.

All sweetness and light, Beethoven suddenly produces an enchanting second subject, a tune that must certainly be classed as one of the happiest he ever wrote. 'It's all right, I didn't mean to hurt you', he seems to be saying, and smiles so charmingly that we forgive the box on the ears he has just given us.

Ex.64

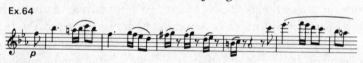

We need to make a cut to the recapitulation for confirmation of my view. It begins exactly as before, the same repetition of the ⌊♩♩ figure, the same embellishment of E♭, the same relaxation followed by the little rising scale, the same duplication of each stage. There is a tiny change of detail in the repetition of Ex. 61, but otherwise everything is identical. The bridge passage (Ex. 62), sets out on the same journey, even appearing to modulate into the dominant. Then comes the stroke of genius.

Ex.65

The whole of Ex. 63 is thrown away—no sad return to square one, no expressive tears, no poignant harmony. Only the irrelevance is preserved, the thumps that had so rudely interrupted our sympathetic response. But their function is now to be like stepping stones that carry us triumphantly to the second subject; what had seemed so out of place is now seen to be very much *in* place, and Beethoven can say with a wink, 'I knew all along I'd find a use for these'. I just cannot accept that had the expressive phrases of Ex. 63 really been intended to be as profound as they at first appear, Beethoven would have been content to eliminate them entirely, not only here but from the rest of the movement as well.

This inevitable diversion has interrupted the continuity of our exploration of the moment, but it is often necessary to glance across several pages before we can understand the whys and wherefores. Let us return to the exposition, where the genial nature of the music seems to me to be amply confirmed by a number of signs of what the immortal W. S. Gilbert would have called 'innocent merriment'. There is a little scale passage of sorts, in which the pianist is expected to cram far too many notes into a bar for comfort, there is a second version of Ex. 64 that seems positively to chuckle, and some mock-angry trills that dissolve into a fountain-like arpeggio that could well have the traditional ping-pong ball bobbing on top of it, waiting to be shot down by an expert marksman. Just near the end of the exposition, Beethoven makes fun of the conventional trill that so often brings the orchestra in at the conclusion of the cadenza in a concerto. The pianist has a couple of tries at establishing a dominant seventh, makes a boss-shot in the left hand (x), puts it right, and flushed with triumph, at last manages to arrive at the long-delayed Bb.

Ex.66

The development begins with Ex. 56 unaltered. One could almost say that the fact that there is no surprise is a surprise in itself. Beethoven then takes the chord progression of Ex. 59, thickens its texture, and moves it outwards with an air of menace towards C minor. By way of experiment, I am now going to effect a marriage between this sonata and the seventh symphony. There is one passage in the symphony notable for an almost overpowering intensity, an effect that is unforgettable in its starkness. It comes in the last movement.

Ex. 67

Now this idea is merely an inversion of the opening figure of this sonata; but here it is treated with genuine ferocity. Let us transplant something of the kind into the context of the sonata.

Ex. 68

My reason for combining elements from these two very different works is to establish a difference of emotional intensity. Without further comment let us see what Beethoven actually did in the sonata.

Ex.69

I tread on dangerous ground here, so let me underline that my conclusions are designed not to diminish Beethoven's stature, but to make him altogether more lovable. One does not have to be ultra-perceptive to realize that the last four bars of Ex. 69 represent a sort of disintegration; the disruption of the rhythm, the almost random appearances of the ⌊♪♪ figure in different areas of the keyboard are both signs of deliberate chaos. The problem is to decide just how seriously it should be taken. I cannot believe that if Beethoven had wished to inspire genuine awe, he would not have used larger resources, similar to the ones I have suggested in Ex. 68. Disintegration there may be, but I believe it is nearer to the classic domestic defence of 'It came to pieces in me 'ands!' than to the splitting of the atom. Looked at as bucolic humour it makes sense, and is entirely characteristic of known aspects of Beethoven's behaviour. Treat it as a serious crisis, and it sadly lacks resource.

The twinkle in the eye as Beethoven immediately restores Ex. 61 (this time in F major), would seem to support my view. He may have knocked the music about a bit, as he did at the end of Ex. 63, but once again the aftermath reveals that it was all in good fun. In the coda there is one delightful moment when pairs of chords advance a step—another step—another—and another, like a child's game. I have heard performances of this work that imposed a deadly seriousness on the entire first movement; they seemed to me a travesty, a denial of all the implications of the notes. There is little surprise that a man so afflicted as Beethoven should be able to write tragic music; what a much greater triumph of the human spirit is revealed when, in one of his darkest hours, he could write something that bubbles over with wit and humour as this delightful sonata does.

The high spirits continue in the Scherzo,[1] which a little surprisingly comes second. Its character, Vivace (lively), is qualified by a warning not to take it too fast. (Allegretto is slower than Allegro.) It is the sort of movement that only Beethoven could have written, full of a rough humour that treads the borderline of slapstick. Let us begin by imagining the theme in a less individual guise.

Ex.70

Charming though this is, it is relatively characterless. Beethoven's treatment is vastly more original, nudging the tune on its way with strong accents in the places where you would least expect them. It isn't often that I allow myself actually to visualize an extra-musical image which is not sanctioned by the composer, but I find it difficult here to resist the idea of being seated in a pony-cart while Beethoven, holding the reins, occasionally digs me in the ribs as he guffaws at some rather school-boyish joke.

Ex.71

The phrase comes twice, being rounded off with a sprightly 'A-men to that'. And now the music goes on tiptoe, its air of stealth being very similar to that of children sneaking up on Grandpa as he is enjoying an afternoon snooze in the garden. The trill should sound like a suppressed giggle.

[1] Unusually in 2/4 time instead of the almost invariable 3/4.

Ex.72

L.H. doubles up an 8va below

We now have a delightful example of musical wit. Beethoven appears to have got stuck on the dominant of F minor (C). How to get back home again seems to be the problem; now in fact it's no real problem at all. The two keys of Ab major and F minor are closely related, as we have seen on p. 20. But Beethoven makes a bit of a mystery about it for reasons that we shall discover later in the movement. For the time being, he comes to a complete halt, ponders awhile, tries the semitone above C (Db), and with an air of triumph shows that it's just the thing he's looking for to get him back home again.

Ex.73

Back trots the first theme, just as before. There's the same little 'A-men', and the same tiptoe phrase (Ex. 72), although this time it's an octave higher. Once again, Beethoven appears to get stuck on the note C. So what are we expecting? A repetition of Ex. 73 of course; Beethoven's rather overdone bewilderment about how to extricate himself from the situation at the end of Ex. 72 has drawn our attention to the point. We remember it, and we remember the earlier solution. What we expect and what we are given are two very different things though; at the quietest moment, indeed after what seems a quite measurable silence, he suddenly bangs down two very loud chords of F major (Ex. 75). The children have let off a firework under Grandpa's deckchair, and the reaction is a frenzy of activity; other isolated explosions follow, but we do not need the word scherzo to tell us that this is all a huge joke. The notes themselves make that clear.

The movement continues with many incidental delights, not the least of which is the descending scale that spans more than

four octaves before it finally brings us exhausted back to Ex. 71.
But the most subtle and purely musical joke is still to come.
Once again, it can only be appreciated in the context of the
movement as a whole, and not as an isolated event. Beethoven
prepares it very carefully by duplicating the events described in
Exx. 71 and 72. Again he goes through the same procedure of
repeating the whole section, again he arrives for the second time
at that C. Two possibilities seem to be available; either he can give
us the D♭ above very quietly, like this:

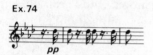

Ex. 74

or we can stand clear for the explosion.

Ex. 75

Unpredictable as ever, Beethoven combines the two ideas,
and gives us two D flats, very loud. There follows the double-
twist that lifts it out of the realms of clowning into high art.
Up to this moment, the D♭ has always been used as a pivot that
would swing us back into A♭ major (see Ex. 73, bars 3–5). Now,
and it is the only time that it happens, the D♭ in its new explosive
form shoots us into the totally unexpected key of G♭ major.

Ex. 76

The practical joke is made to serve an intellectual purpose.
The sudden crash that Haydn had amused himself with in the
slow movement of the Surprise symphony, is here given a new
function, one which is purely musical in its effect. After these

shocks, the end of the movement is sheer delight, a tiptoe exit
that makes something new out of the oldest cliché in music.

The third movement is something of a throwback, a Menuetto,
the last that Beethoven was to use in a major piano work. (The
'Tempo di Menuetto' movement in the little G major sonata,
Op. 49 No. 2 is not in fact a minuet at all, but a rondo; anyway,
it is an adaptation of an earlier composition.) It shows Beethoven
in his most beguiling mood, with a beautiful singing tune presented
in terms of the utmost simplicity. The only touch of pathos is
introduced by an occasional C♮ (x), though its effect is nearer
to the sweeter pangs of love than any real despair.

Ex.77

The implied harmony in this passage is echoed in the second
part of the unusual Trio (or middle section of a minuet), which
is based on a pattern of what can only be described as sedate skips.
It is this Trio that Saint-Saëns used as the basis of a two-piano
work called 'Variations on a theme of Beethoven', its combination
of simplicity and easily remembered landmarks serving his purpose
admirably. The movement ends with a brief Coda, based on the
principal feature of Ex. 77, though this time there is something
nearer to genuine pathos in its presentation.

Any possible tinge of sorrow is instantly dispelled by the
galloping finale, a movement that takes off like a potential
Derby-winner and only slackens its pace once—unnervingly
near to the winning-post I may say. Czerny tells of an incident
in the summer of 1802 when Beethoven saw a rider gallop past

the windows of the house in the country where he was staying. The regular beat of the horse's hooves supposedly gave him the idea for the finale of Op. 31 No. 2.

Ex.78

The indications Allegretto and *p* make this into a very leisurely gallop, and I can't help wondering if Czerny's recollection was not at fault; it seems much more likely that the music inspired by the incident was the finale of this sonata. It was inevitable that it should acquire the nickname of *La Chasse* or the Hunt. The suggestion of pounding hooves and hunting horns is irresistible.

Ex.79

Superficially, there are resemblances between this and the second movement of Op. 109, although the later work has much greater variety, and considerably more seriousness of purpose. There is one comparison worth making though for the indications it gives of Beethoven's greater awareness of craftsmanship as he grew more mature. In this finale we find one passage in which he repeats the same note a number of times. The harmony beneath remains virtually unaltered.

Ex.80

In Op. 109 we find a rather similar idea of repeated notes, but now with a much more interesting treatment.

Ex. 81

However, it is only fair to say that much of the exhilaration that we derive from listening to the last movement of Op. 31 No. 3 is caused by the non-stop drive of the rhythm and the elemental appeal of the harmony.

The central section of the movement has some quite impressive modulations, but again I think there is a danger, in the light of our knowledge of late Beethoven, that we may be tempted to make the teacup a sight too large for this particular storm. Here is that 'extreme boisterousness' of which Ries spoke, and Beethoven plays a cruel joke on the pianist on the final page when prodigiously rapid crossing of the hands is called for. Twice in the last few bars the music comes to an abrupt halt, like a horse being urged towards a jump only to refuse at the very last stride. A little wistfully, Beethoven turns away and then, suddenly resolved, dashes off the last few bars.

Now I can well imagine that my rather frivolous approach to this sonata may cause some exasperation to many sincere lovers of Beethoven's music. If I have committed what seem to be heresies, let me defend them by saying this. We know from the evidence of Beethoven's associates that he was given to outbursts of boisterous humour; their musical manifestation is evident in many individual movements, bagatelles, the scherzos of the symphonies, and of course in parts of the quartets. In its more obvious forms, this humour is unmistakable; this sonata shows humour of a more subtle kind. So much stress has been laid on the near-divine quality of Beethoven that we tend to feel something almost sacrilegious in treating him as a human being. Yet he was the greater man for being able to laugh as well as weep; surely he would want us to share his moods rather than to deify him.

CHAPTER VI

BEETHOVEN

Opp. 57 and 111—a comparison

Op. 57 in F minor. (The Appassionata.) Date uncertain, though sketches appear as early as 1804. Published February 1807 by Bureau des Arts et d'Industrie in Vienna; dedicated to Count Franz von Brunswick, brother to the Countesses Therese and Josephine with both of whom Beethoven was enamoured, and either of whom might be the unknown woman who never received the three impassioned love letters that Beethoven wrote, but then concealed in a secret drawer.[1] The nickname, Appassionata, was supplied by the publisher Cranz, who was also responsible for calling Op. 28 the Pastoral.

1. Allegro assai. 2 Andante con moto. (Variations), leading to 3. Allegro ma non troppo—ultimately Presto.

Op. 111 in C minor. The final sonata. Composed January 1822; first published April 1823, Schlesinger, Berlin and Paris. Dedicated to his patron and beloved pupil, the Archduke Rudolph of Austria, although according to Grove the dedication was added by the publisher. Only two important piano works written after this were the Diabelli Variations and the Bagatelles Op. 126.

1. Maestoso, leading to Allegro con brio e appassionato.
2. Arietta; Adagio molto, semplice e cantabile. (Actually a set of variations.)
There is no third movement.

ALTHOUGH, as we have seen, Op. 31 begins with a chord that is enigmatic and non-committal, it was not destined to establish a precedent. Each one of the remaining sonatas begins

[1] See *Letters of Beethoven*, trans. Emily Anderson, No. 373 Vol. 1, Macmillan, and other sources.

with a theme which establishes the tonic key without possibility of doubt, all, that is, save for Op. 111, whose opening phrase is cast in a truly heroic mould. It begins with a magnificent gesture.

Ex. 82

One feels that Beethoven positively resents the limitations imposed on him by the pianist only having two hands; a chord such as the one marked with a bridge ⌐‾‾‾⌐ covers a span of more than three octaves, yet one senses that ideally, Beethoven would like it to be played as one huge chord.

Now the opening harmony, xx, is what is known as a diminished seventh, and it is a chord that has a special function in music. It invariably has implications of drama, even melodrama. When, in the days of the silent cinema, the pianist was called upon to accompany moments of villany—('In vain Mabel struggled in his clutches; blackhearted Rudolph clasped her in his arms and dragged her screaming to the foot of the stairs')— he would inevitably use diminished sevenths by the handful. Over the years this particular chord must have accompanied more attempted rapes than any other harmony. Why should this be so? Why should great composers and pit pianists alike use this chord to convey drama? What intrinsic quality does it have that makes it so different from any other?

To a composer of the pre-Wagner era, the diminished seventh was a cross-roads chord; it represents a moment of choice, when a number of roads lie open before him and he must decide which one to take. A diminished seventh is a modulating device of great flexibility, as the chart below demonstrates.

Fig. 3

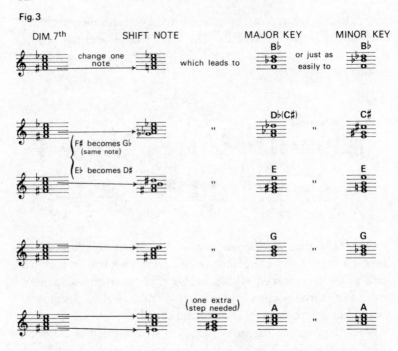

The single chord in the left-hand column opens the door to ten different keys shown in the two right-hand columns. Small wonder that Samuel Butler described it as 'the Clapham Junction of music'. The moment that a composer uses such a chord he poses a question to the listener: 'Which road shall I take to put an end to this suspense?' Suspense, then, is the factor that is shared by the awe-inspiring opening of Op. 111 or the inane accompaniment to Mabel's tribulations at the foot of the stairs.

The introduction to this sonata is like a cross-roads itself, a mountain pass, overcast with black clouds shot through with lightning. Above all, though, is this suggestion of seeking the way out—which path is the right one? Which chord will ultimately resolve the torment and confusion which the opening phrases convey so eloquently? Surely this sequence is a search, even to the moment of decision at the end.

Ex.83

That final chord resolves our doubts; Beethoven may drag out the suspense still further, which indeed he does most movingly, but it was the first of all those tentative explorations of key to have established a clear dominant harmony. Where there is a dominant, a tonic will surely follow in due course, and after so dark a prologue, it must inevitably be C minor. As a prologue, its purpose is remarkably similar to the first page of the Pathétique sonata, Op. 13; both introductions set the scene for tragedy, both lead into movements of great turbulence and intensity. Few comparisons give us a clearer idea of how vast a change had come over the language in the space of twenty-five years.

Logically we might expect the Appassionata to have been written half-way between these two works, but curiously enough it comes much sooner after the Pathétique than one would imagine. Op. 13 dates from 1798; it was a mere six years after this that the first sketches of Op. 57 appear. Its composition must have been an almost frightening experience for Beethoven. He had unleashed forces that were nearly beyond his control, and it's scarcely surprising that he took a couple of years to find how to handle them.

The first essential difference between the start of Op. 111 and the start of the Appassionata is that the earlier work, for all its essentially romantic character, still observes the time-honoured convention of beginning with a clear indication of tonality. In this it is no different from Op. 2 No. 1, the first of the thirty-two sonatas.

Ex. 84

Here we have an arpeggio of F minor stated in crisp, classical terms in a language that was essentially the same as Haydn's—indeed, the sonata is dedicated to Haydn. The Appassionata also begins with an arpeggio in F minor.

Ex. 85

The same arpeggio maybe, but what a difference these dark evocative tones convey. The wide spacing of the hands, the more varied rhythm, the almost imperceptible merging into harmony, the trill that dissolves the phrase into silence—the whole treatment is infinitely more Romantic. Yet it still acknowledges the classical need for the clear definition of tonality at the start of a work. Beethoven's technique, based on the traditional precepts of key-relationships, tells him to use a theme that establishes the tonal centre of F minor; but his emotional inclination is towards something much more mysterious. That air of mystery he now attains by immediately repeating the phrase in G♭ major, only a slight

★ I once heard Cortot describe this as 'The moon rising through the trees. . . .' No comment!

change of pitch, but an enormous change in other respects. Not only is the immediate denial of the carefully established key of F minor disturbing, but the release of tension involved in shifting from minor to major has its effect as well. He retraces his steps, back to F minor, building suspense with ominous drum-beats in the left hand. It is the hush before the storm. The music, which up to this point has seemed to be veiled in mist, is suddenly torn apart, first by a vivid lightning flash, and then by thunderous chords.

Ex. 86

This is a passage which is extremely difficult to bring off convincingly in performance, the alternations of soft–loud– soft–loud being so rapid, and the *fortissimo* chords tending to make the pianist sound as though he is merely having a tantrum. This indeed could be a legitimate interpretation of Beethoven's intentions. As I see it, he is beating his head against a wall here, which is frustrating at the best of times. What he is really trying to do, although he is unaware of it, is to make the journey from Op. 2 No. 1 to Op. 111 by a quicker route than natural development would allow. The goal is there, but as yet indistinctly seen. Time and again in this sonata, we can see intimations of things to come; nor are they only later developments in his own music. The noble romanticism of the second subject of Op. 57 bears more than a suggestion of Schumann.

Ex. 87

As for this marvellously turbulent passage:

Ex.88

Op.57

surely it sows the seeds of the finale of Chopin's sonata in B minor.

Ex.89

Chopin
Op.58
IV

They may not look all that similar on paper, but the emotional content is very close, and the actual 'feel' in the hand is a likeness which any player must appreciate.

The start of the Appassionata is curiously elusive and fragmentary; by comparison, Op. 111 is as strong as a rock. From its Homeric introduction emerges an immensely arresting theme,[1] the more dramatic for the roll of thunder which precedes it.

Ex.90

Op.111

Now curiously enough, Beethoven had had a premonition of this shape in the Appassionata. The very last section of the finale is a frenzied dance based on this pattern. (I quote its second appearance.)

[1] It had first appeared in the sketch-books some twenty years earlier, in the key of F♯ minor, as part of a violin sonata.

Ex. 91

The relationship is fairly easy to spot, in spite of differences of notation and key. The differences between the two works become most marked when we see how Beethoven continues from such similar beginnings. In the Appassionata we find what in my opinion is the one unsatisfactory part of the composition. Even in masterly hands, I find this ending something of an anti-climax, a little too near to the traditional Gipsy Dance that appears so often in the less probable nineteenth-century operas.

In Op. 111, those same notes are used as the seed from which the most wonderful developments spring. The music is no less tigerish in its intensity, but gains immeasurably from its greater intellectual power. Although the first movement is extremely economical in themes, there is a remarkable freedom about it. It far transcends the bounds of normal sonata form, having elements of fugue, fantasy and inspired improvisation in it. Yet it can also at a stretch be analysed in terms of normal first and second subjects if you wish.

As in so many of the late works, the thing most calculated to confuse the listener is the sudden changes of mood that are so characteristic. Beethoven demands a very rapid and flexible response from his audience; the music is torn apart by conflicting emotions. The person who is unable to adjust quickly enough tends to give up and turn to a nice quiet nocturne or waltz; at least one knows where one is. In this movement, which is like a sort of musical equivalent to *King Lear*, there is much that is stormy, but also there are moments of great pathos.

Ex. 92

Here again we have a fascinating instance of the two-way process of composition that I have discussed already on pp. 36-37. The chords in Ex. 92 have 'softer' implications about them, not just in terms of volume but emotion; driven by the storm though he is, Beethoven clutches at them in passing, and automatically, because they are chords of that particular quality, the tension is diminished. It is a moment every real composer knows, when the music takes on a life of its own, and goes in a direction one hadn't bargained for. There is something terrifying about the way in which this moment of compassion is obliterated by a great cascade of notes that seem to come tearing out of the sky, sweeping all before them.

In the development, Beethoven tries to cage his tiger. Usually, the development section implies a loosening-up, an expansion of material. After such a tempest as we have ridden out here, he tries instead to compress, to impose the disciplines of strict form and counterpoint on the unruly material we have heard so far. He takes Ex. 90, the principal theme of the allegro, and binds it tight with academic cords. Ex. 93 shows the framework, leaving out the inessentials.

Ex. 93

Within ten bars, things have got out of hand again. I am convinced that Beethoven originally planned a longer section of controlled counterpoint here, but the gesture proves as ineffectual as a single professor trying to quell a student riot. Any suggestion of fugal treatment is swept away by sheer force. The hammer-blows of Ex. 90 strike again and again until the immense central climax is reached.

Surprisingly, the movement ends quietly, perhaps in preparation for the unearthly serenity of the second movement, perhaps because the driving force finally burns itself out. Certainly there is a strange effect of disintegration towards the end as Ex. 90 breaks into fragments.

Ex.94

This last phrase, in conjunction with its swift moving left hand, is an uncanny anticipation of the dying fall that comes so near the end of Chopin's Revolutionary study. But where Chopin flings the music into one last gesture of defiance, Beethoven's movement sinks at last into an uneasy rest. It is interesting that the first movement of Op. 57 ends the same way—with disintegration, followed by an unexpected descent into darkness.

The motive may well be the same in both sonatas, for in each case, from the storm-racked turbulence of the first movement we are suddenly translated into a world of extraordinary peace. Both movements are sets of variations, both are in a major key, both have themes of notable stillness, though in Op. 57, Beethoven cautions the performer against adopting too slow a tempo. The theme in Op. 57 is more a sequence of harmonies than a melody; had he been so inclined, Beethoven might have thought of it as a sort of Chaconne, though it would then have required three beats in a bar instead of two. There is a tendency for occasional movements in the bass to attract our attention, and I think this is proof that Beethoven did not want us to become too absorbed in the melodic aspect of the music. The variations throughout are designed to stress the harmonic nature of the theme.

In a rather earlier period, there had been a great vogue for a type of variation known as 'doubles'. Handel's Harmonious Blacksmith is a good example, with each variation sticking to the same harmonic framework, but with a progressively increasing number of notes allotted to each beat. Theoretically, the theme is in units of one beat; in the first variation you divide each unit by two; variation two has three notes per beat; next we find four notes to a beat, then six, and eight for the last, thus bringing the house down with an increasingly dazzling display of virtuosity.

These two slow movements are both very elaborate examples of this long-established technique. The Op. 57 movement is less varied in mood, but this, no doubt, is because there is still a vigorous third movement to come. The variations are also somewhat more strict in their adherence to the original theme, but that is largely the result of concentrating on the elaboration of harmony rather than the extension of melody. It is here that the movements begin to differ.

A composer of variations may decide on several courses of action; he may choose to adhere strictly to the original framework, as for instance Brahms does in his Variations on a theme by Handel for the greater part of the work. He may take one small aspect of the theme and develop it freely in its own right, as Rachmaninoff does in the famous D♭ Variation XVIII of his Paganini Rhapsody. He may concentrate on a rhythm, a sequence of chords, a technical trick such as constructing a canon, or even introduce a totally extra-musical idea as Elgar does in the Enigma variations. Beethoven's technique in Op. 111 is a remarkable instance of musical growth. The theme itself is a mere sixteen bars long, though, as was the usual custom, both halves are repeated. Yet although the music continues to evolve with this limitation very much in mind, one has a feeling of an immense span unfolding. The 'units' in the Diabelli variations for instance remain very clear cut for the most part, even though Beethoven's ingenuity in dealing with a trite little idea is staggering. But in this sonata, apart from one frenetic outburst whose savage syncopations give a strangely demonic quality, the rest of the movement remains extraordinarily still, even though the page is black with notes. It is a style of writing that occurs quite often in late Beethoven, when he marries a broad slow-moving tune to an accompaniment of great activity. Demi-semi-quavers and trills make the music glitter with their abundance; listening, I remember the Biblical phrase about the Spirit of God moving over the waters, water in constant, rippling movement, reflecting the light of a million stars, teeming with life and creation, yet contained in one all-embracing and infinite intelligence.

CHAPTER VII

TOWARDS SCHUMANN

Some thoughts on Beethoven's Sonata in
A Major Op. 101

Sonata No. 28 in A major, Op. 101. Finished early in 1816. Published 1817 by Steiner of Vienna. Dedicated to the Baroness Dorothea von Ertmann, herself an accomplished pianist. Beethoven admired her playing enough to give her the nickname, 'Cecilia', after the patron Saint of music. Despite his contempt for patronage, some of his truest friends were aristocrats; it is said that when the Baroness was demented with grief over the death of one of her children, Beethoven saved her reason by playing to her.

It was for this sonata, not Op. 106, that he first invented the term Hammerklavier, in preference to the Italian word Pianoforte. His nationalistic fervour briefly extended to instructions about tempo and style of playing, but he was soon to revert to Italian again.

FACTS HAVE THEIR PLACE in the field of scholarship, and, since my own mind is singularly empty of them, I am grateful to the many excellent scholars who have consigned facts to print; and on whose store of knowledge I am entirely dependant when it comes to matters of dates, places and the like. But sometimes convictions are better than facts; sometimes it is more important to believe than to know. It is in this spirit that I say that I am quite sure that I know which Beethoven sonata Schumann loved the most, even though I haven't a word of documentary evidence to prove it. If I was a scholar, and had the sort of conscientious dedication that goes with a scholarly mind, I would settle down to a happy couple of years' research through the whole of Schumann's writings (which were considerable) in order to find some confirmation of my belief. Curiously enough, I don't really care all that much whether such confirmation exists or not; I would go further and say that it doesn't even matter to me if Schumann wrote somewhere that his favourite Beethoven sonata was a different one altogether, since my reason for being interested is not to prove a small historical fact but to demonstrate a large artistic truth. This truth is that there is one sonata of Beethoven's in which we can find so many anticipations of Schumann's mature style that I am utterly fascinated by it. It is almost as if, by one of those miraculous shifts in time so favoured by writers of science fiction, Beethoven had been able to peer into the future and look at some of Schumann's music. (One fact here by the way, confirmed by a quick look in a book of reference—Schumann was seventeen when Beethoven died in 1827, so there is no chance that Beethoven could have seen any of his music.)

Now, it is one of the main contentions of this book that Beethoven grew increasingly dissatisfied with sonata form towards the end of his life. All the late sonatas seem to be moving towards something far more rhapsodic, more loosely constructed. (The slow movement of the Hammerklavier sonata even moves into what might be called the Mahlerian time-scale.) He expressed this discontent in several ways: one, as in the first movement of Op. 109, was to preserve solely the 'idea' of contrast that was originally exemplified by first and second subjects, but to pursue it to an extreme—contrast of tempo, emotional content, style of writing, contrast of opposites too violent to be acceptable in a normal sonata form context. Another way was to jettison even contrast, to make a whole movement more unified so that while there would be some variety of theme, the essential mood would remain constant. Both movements of Op. 78, the finale of Op. 90 and the first movement of this sonata, Op. 101, are the clearest instances of this trend; it begins to move the sonata as a form much nearer to what, for want of a better term, might be called Mood Music. Considerations of sentiment begin to govern considerations of intellect. The third, and most unkind, way of expressing his frustration was to write thoroughly unpianistic music that allowed its intellectual demands to override all thought of practicality. The Hammerklavier is the supreme example— as is the Grosse Fuge in the quartet repertoire—but the last movement of this twenty-eighth sonata is vastly inconsiderate to the pianist.

If Beethoven allowed his feelings for the Baroness Dorothea to be expressed in the first movement of Op. 101, they must have been tender indeed, for the music begins in the most meltingly beautiful fashion.

Ex. 95

I have put his indications of performance into English, since, if he was so determined to play a nationalist game, I don't see why I shouldn't be allowed to play as well. But it is interesting as an indication of his dread of sentimentality that even here, when he asks for 'heartfelt expression' (*innigsten Empfindung*), he should feel the need to qualify it by the seemingly contradictory *Etwas lebhaft*, or 'somewhat lively'. One suspects that had these notes actually been written by Schumann, he would not have betrayed such qualms.

The music continues in this lyrical and tender mood. The rare indications of *f* seem to call for the full tone of a string orchestra rather than an aggressive impact. The wide-spaced harmony is one significant pointer to the full romantic style of Schumann or Brahms. The spacing of a chord is one of its most important attributes. As the keyboard itself acquired a wider compass, composers tended to open out the harmony. The so-called Alberti bass that occurs so frequently in Haydn and Mozart, was merely extended to cover a wider range of the

keyboard in Chopin's hands. The effect is

richer, since the notes have a greater variety of colour. When Stravinsky began his Symphony of Psalms with this version of the chord of E minor:

he was simply taking a remarkably fresh look at the familiar notes E G B which had been in use for centuries.

The spacing of Beethoven's harmony is a study in itself. When, for instance, he transposes the opening melody of the slow movement of Op. 13 up an octave, he realizes the need to compensate for the relative thinness of the middle range of the keyboard. If you try playing the first phrase an octave higher with exactly the same lay-out as when it first appears, you will hear what I mean. So far as I am aware, the interval of a tenth

simply does not exist in the piano music of Haydn and Mozart, yet Beethoven uses it as early as Op. 2 No. 3 (bar 56). (I don't count the 'scrambled' tenths in the first movement of Op. 2 No. 2—they are the result of counterpoint, not harmony.) What in my opinion is the single most beautiful chord that Beethoven ever committed to paper is to be found in the first movement of Op. 109. It is instructive to compare it with another magical chord, the one that begins the fourth piano concerto. Here they are, side by side.

If the words Classical and Romantic have any significance with regard to taste, one could say that these two chords, each perfect in its own right, epitomize the difference. It is the use of tenths however which gives the second chord its particularly romantic quality, the F♯ → A♯ and then the A♯ → C♯. Schumann, the German Romantic *par excellence*, constantly exploits chords of the tenth. Look in bars 3 and 4 of Ex. 95, and you will find the melody itself stated in tenths. As I have suggested, the whole language of the sonata is moving towards Schumann.

One of Schumann's most notable idiosyncrasies is an obsession with tied notes, notes held over silently from a previous beat. Here is a typical passage from his magnificent Fantasy in C, Op. 17.

Ex. 96

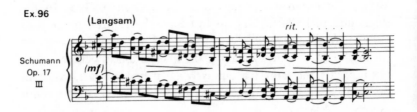

With a prodigious amount of sniffing and nodding of the head, it's perfectly feasible for the pianist to show an audience where the beats actually lie, although they are all silent. Equally, it's possible to disregard the subtle implications of Schumann's notation and produce a sound like this, which, theoretically, has exactly the same note values.

Ex.97

I feel that the slight disorientation of the beat that Schumann conveys by his way of writing is an indication of 'beatless-ness', a deliberately contrived effect of anti-rhythm, totally different from what we normally think of as syncopation. If Ex. 96 seems perverse in its notation, Ex. 97 is downright dull. Schumann's version also carries some implications of a slight emotional tension, a quickening of the heartbeat which is difficult to bring off, but worth trying for. At the very least, his notation could be said to convey 'Don't just play the notes—do *something*!'

In Beethoven's Op. 101 we find exactly the same technique, employed, I would surmise, for just the same purpose. Here is the rhythm only (alike in both hands), of one passage.

L.H. drops out

Again the same effect of 'beatless-ness', giving a beautifully spontaneous feel to the occasional wisp of melody that emerges from what an orchestral musician would regard as 'viola territory'.

Ex.98

Op.101 (pp)

(Notice the very subtle difference between the two left hand melodies, the first one with its dipping quavers on the second beat, the second aiming more directly at its peak.) For Beethoven to use this rhythm was very unusual; he seems, as I have suggested,

to have hit upon one of the hallmarks of Schumann's style.
I stress Schumann at the expense of the other Romantics simply
because it was a trick he used much more frequently than his
contemporaries. For instance, when Chopin began his F major
Ballade, he did *not* choose to start like this,

Ex.99

but used the more normal rhythm, without ties.

I should be making out a poor case if this was the only evidence
I was to produce in support of my argument that this sonata is not
only a gateway to Romanticism, but to Schumann in particular.
There is a stronger link to be established in the next movement.
This is as unique in Beethoven's output as the first movement is,
though in a different way. It's a March of immense vigour,
characterized by an obsessional use of one rhythm.

Ex.100

This driving rhythm continues relentlessly for more than
two-thirds of the entire movement. Now anybody who has even
read through a fair sample of Schumann's work, however ineptly,
will recognize this as one of his most typical rhythms. To quote
three examples, the final movement of the Etudes Symphoniques:

Ex.101

Kreisleriana, No. 5:

Ex.102

or the second movement of the Op. 17 Fantasy:

Ex.103

In each of these examples, the rhythm shown is a persistent and outstanding feature, continuing for long stretches at a time. This is the point—not the rhythm itself, but the persistence with which it is pursued. I know of no other movement in Beethoven that employs so similar a technique of composition.[1] There are other Schumann tricks too, the piling of entries on top of each other, the way that phrases interlock, the crossing of hands, all perhaps best revealed in this climax.

Ex.104

The instruction *dolce* (sweetly), when the left hand is suddenly

---

[1] I refer to piano music. The Grosse Fuge comes to mind as another example of dotted rhythm. The 'Turkish March' section of the Ninth Symphony also has a surprisingly Schumannesque quality, but is scarcely a fair comparison.

projected into the pianistic stratosphere is typical of Beethoven's inhumanity to man, when it comes to questions of practicality. But the whole 'feel' of this passage in the hand is astonishingly close to Schumann in texture.

At this point, the impatient reader may well be muttering, 'So what?' I've made the point, but is the point worth making? My justification for devoting a chapter to it is that I am always fascinated by the inevitability of certain developments in music. There *is* a sort of pre-destination at work; for instance, like it or not, the twentieth century had to come; its course was pre-ordained from the moment that Schoenberg discovered that he could not outdo Wagner on his own ground. It is like those endless 'begat' chapters in the Bible—'and Haydn begat Beethoven, and Beethoven begat Brahms, and Liszt begat Bartók, and Wagner begat Schoenberg, and Schoenberg begat Berg', and so on. But it isn't often that one can put a finger so surely on an actual work that links two composers so widely differing in their fundamental approach to music. Essentially, Schumann and Beethoven belonged to two completely different worlds united only by the Germanic tie. Schumann was far more drawn to a literary or pictorial conception of music's function; atmosphere and emotion were much higher priorities with him than structure. His admiration for Beethoven was enormous, but his natural inclination was to use very different forms. When, therefore, I lay so much stress on the Schumann-like qualities of Op. 101, it is not my intention to suggest that Schumann copied it or was even consciously influenced by it. What concerns me is not Schumann looking back, but Beethoven looking forward. If one says flatly that Beethoven's life-work was to bridge the gulf between Haydn and the mid-nineteenth-century Romantics, it is an over-simplification, suggesting that the gulf was one of time alone. It was not; it was an immense change of outlook involving the rejection of the classical aesthetic, and the acceptance of a more personal, involved approach to composition. The whole of the next chapter is devoted to the work that best symbolizes that journey.

CHAPTER VIII

BEETHOVEN

Op. 110 in A♭ Major

Composed in December 1821, the penultimate sonata, and the only complete work to be written in that year, the rest of his time being devoted to the Missa Solemnis[1] and the Ninth Symphony. The sonata bears no dedication, although at one time Beethoven appears to have considered dedicating it to his pupil Ries, or to a Frau Brentano.[2] In the event, it was published by Schlesinger in 1822. Beethoven claimed (to his friend Anton Schindler) that he had written the last three sonatas 'in a single breath', in order to quiet the apprehension of his friends about his mental condition, which was growing ever more eccentric. But this was a downright lie, since Op. 109 clearly belongs to 1820, and was actually published before work on Op. 110 had begun.

1. Moderato cantabile molto espressivo. 2. Allegro molto. 3. Adagio ma non troppo—Recitativo—several rapid changes of tempo over a few bars—Adagio, ma non troppo (Arioso dolente). 3(a). Fuga; allegro, ma non troppo—return to the tempo of the Arioso—return to tempo of Fuga—a gradual increase of speed to the end.

THE LANGUAGE OF MUSIC, like any other language, is capable of expressing things simply or obscurely; but since few people are capable of 'thinking' in musical abstractions, the average listener tends to enjoy most those pieces that have the power to suggest things outside music. Tchaikovsky's symphonies are easier to listen to than those of Beethoven

---

[1] By then more than a year overdue for the occasion for which it was supposed to be written.

[2] Mother of Maximiliana, dedicatee of Op. 109.

because they are more likely to bring imaginary pictures into the mind; a cavalry charge, a gipsy dance, a vast expanse of woods and lakes, the dead ashes of burned love-letters, death, love, darkness, loneliness. While I'm all for identification with the music, I cannot help deprecating this response, except when it is sanctioned by the composer. Yet there exists a great demand to know what a work *means*, to unravel the secrets in some way. Precisely because we find the emotional content of music easier to grasp than its intellectual aspects, we fall back on the prop of analysis, feeling that some sort of illumination should follow, once we know that the nice bit on the clarinet is the recapitulation of the second subject in the tonic key. It was Mendelssohn who said, 'The thoughts which are expressed to me by music . . . are not too indefinite to be put into words, but on the contrary, too definite'. This slightly enigmatic remark makes sense once we accept that the musical language exists in its own right, and that it is as foolish to expect it to speak to us in verbal concepts, as it would be to play a tune to the grocer over the telephone and expect him to translate it into an order for the week's provisions.

Before we examine this sonata in detail, let us look at one phrase. It is by no means new in Beethoven's work; as early as Op. 10 No. 1, the piano sonata in C minor, we find this fragment.

Ex.105

The same shape occurs in a rather smoother guise in the String Quartet, Op. 18 No. 5.

Ex.106

Two years later, in 1802, it emerged from Beethoven's subconscious in yet another form, as part of the Violin Sonata, Op. 30 No. 3;

Ex.107

while in 1808, it reappeared yet again in the Trio, Op. 70 No. 2.

Ex.108

The only thing remarkable about these resemblances is not their similarity but the completely different ways in which they evolve. There can be little doubt though that the most perfect version of this useful and versatile pattern is to be found starting in the fifth bar of this sonata.

Ex.109

Op. 110

The accompaniment Beethoven gives us to this exquisite arch of melody would seem at first glance to be a cliché of unbelievable banality. Can the mature master really be satisfied with this relic of childhood days?

Ex.110

How are we to accept the same basis that 'Chopsticks' is built on, in a work which all authorities agree to be one of the most sublime ever written for piano?

In explanation, I would turn back to verbal language. One of the most profound and moving lines in the whole of English literature is made up of words of the utmost simplicity:

To be or not to be . . .

It would be hard to invent a phrase that said more with

less effort; it is not 'better' to say, 'To exist or to stop existing', or, 'TheproblemisthatIcan'tdecidewhethertogoonmaking
theseawfuldecisionsortoputanendtoitallbydoingmyselfin'.   The
simplicity of utterance lends dignity to the thought expressed;
so here, Beethoven, by daring to be simple, succeeds in being
profound.

Despite its confusing, indeterminate number of movements,
there is an overwhelming unity about Op. 110, a unity which
Beethoven achieves in a number of subtle ways, as we shall
see. We can afford to make a very detailed study of this sonata,
since it might literally be described as the 'work of a lifetime'.
To my mind, it sums up the whole purpose of Beethoven's life;
in this one work, we find a perfect symbol of his journey from
Classicism to Romanticism, terms which I use not to indicate
two periods of time, but rather attitudes of mind.

The work begins with a serene phrase which Beethoven
specifically asks us to play 'lovingly'. Yet as early as the third bar,
it hesitates, coming to rest on a trill before continuing into Ex. 109.
It must rank with the start of the Fourth Piano Concerto as one
of the most poetic openings of all time.

Ex.111

These brief opening bars are much more than a mere prologue,
more even than a first subject; they are, as we shall discover,
the source from which many later events are to spring.

The music goes on its way, lyrical, sustained and tranquil in
spirit. Suddenly, and to our perplexity, Beethoven embarks on a
whole series of glistening arpeggios. What place do these digital
exercises have in such a meditation?

Ex.112

The clue is to be found in 112a, which shows us that these are far from digital exercises, but a variation on Ex. 111. On a modern piano it demands extreme delicacy of touch to achieve the filigree effect that must be neither too clouded nor too sparkling. Meantime, the left hand sketches in suggestions of harmony, mere props for the fragile structure above. The figures climb higher, up to the topmost note of Beethoven's piano, the high C. From this improbable peak, where sound has begun to lose substance, an almost languorous melody drifts down, its shape growing more definite as it descends. No sooner has it coalesced into actual chords than it begins to climb again, the feeling of ascent being intensified by the now-spread chords, which seem to be reaching out towards the unattainable. It is Beethoven's masterly way of disguising the fact that he has already overshot the note that he now wishes us to feel is the summit. He is aiming for the top B♭, a tone lower than the previous high C. But the approach is so skilfully done, with descending trills in the left hand widening the gap between the hands, that we have no sense of anticlimax.

Ex.113

This last dramatic plunge downwards through more than two octaves is another way of emphasizing the climactic nature of the top B♭; the music seems literally to have broken apart. Three more brief ascents bring us indeed to the top C, now attained in such a way as to seem the real climax of the movement so far. The music gently unwinds and settles down into a dominant harmony that has every appearance of leading us to a traditional double-bar, with the consequent repeat of the opening exposition.

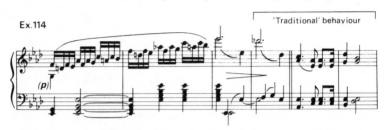

Ex.114

'Traditional' behaviour

✳Beethoven has grown impatient with such traditions by now, and in Opp. 101, 109 and 110 he abandons them. It is perhaps significant that these three sonatas all have first movements of an unusually lyrical nature; in the more demanding first movements of Opp. 106 and 111, he still preserves the custom of repeating the exposition.

What he actually does in Op. 110 is to shift the bass down to Db at the same time as the top line, effectively destroying any suggestion that the Db is merely a rather feeble dominant seventh, and giving it the strength to move us into a new key, F minor. This change is underlined by a crescendo that goes against the grain; just as the pianist's instincts cry out to play with even more sentiment, Beethoven forces him to push on. (Ex. 115 picks up from bar 3 of Ex. 114.)

Ex.115

✳ Suddenly, as though Beethoven realizes how contrary he is being by forcing this music to go against its nature, he relents, and the rest of the remarkable short development is all meditative, an oft-repeated contemplation of the opening phrase of the sonata, tinged with melancholy and subtly changing direction till, through several related keys, it brings us back to A♭ major.

In the world of tonal music, there is a deep underlying sense of 'rightness', a feeling of proportion that is akin to architecture. There's some interesting evidence to be discovered about this if we compare the development section of this Beethoven sonata with the very different sounding development of Mozart's K.457. (See Chapter III.) Where Beethoven is contemplative, Mozart is turbulent; but both in essence are disguising a sequence of *harmonies* by presenting them as *melodies*. On the face of it, the emotional content and melodic outline of these two examples could not be much further apart.

Ex.116
Mozart K.457

Beethoven Op.110

Yet once we look at these bars as alternations of harmony, they begin to seem extraordinarily alike; the details may differ, but the procedure, and the sort of logic that governs it, is virtually the same. Here, first, is a sort of ground-plan:

Fig. 4

Mozart:	F minor	Dominant of G minor	G minor	Dominant of C minor	C minor	Dominant of C minor
Beethoven:	F minor	Dominant of F minor	F minor	Dominant of D♭ major	D♭ major	Dominant of D♭ major

Using the most similar placings for these harmonies on the keyboard, we would find something like this:

Ex.117

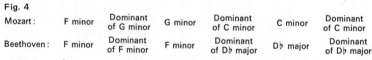

Mozart:

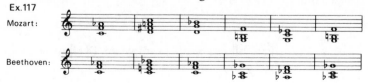

Beethoven:

The resemblances are obvious when presented in this skeletonic form. My only reason for revealing them is to show the instinctive sense of harmonic balance that seems to have been developed in the classical composer, even when he was writing in an impassioned vein. Poles apart emotionally, the two sonatas both have developments of exceptional concentration, devoted virtually to one idea; both are also concerned with tonic-dominant relationships, the 'twist' being to turn to an unexpected new dominant from time to time so as to be able to move forward to a new tonal centre.

By these gradual steps, Beethoven gently steers us back to Ab major; this time, the opening phrase is accompanied by the exercise-like figure which had seemed so curious an interruption when it first appeared as Ex. 112; its function is now made plain. The movement proceeds without drama, its outlines remarkably clear and orthodox. One problem occurs when Beethoven finds himself climbing to a non-existent note. Owing to a necessary transposition, he is driven towards a top C♯ instead of the top C he had reached earlier. Since such a note did not exist on any piano of his time,[1] he was compelled suddenly to plunge the music down an octave; ineptly performed, it can sound a bit clumsy, though in the right hands it has the effect of enriching the texture. The only other point that demands attention is a slight darkening of the mood in the very final bars of the movement.

Ex. 118

The repercussions of this phrase are destined to extend further than we think.

The scherzo that follows is an example of Beethoven at his most terse; at first glance, the music seems almost naive in its

[1] We now have an entire octave more than Beethoven's piano had in its upper register.

simplicity, and it's quite possible to imagine a piece suitable for a child beginner, with a melody on these lines.

Ex.119

From such fundamentals Beethoven builds a movement of tremendous nervous energy. One gets the impression of explosive forces barely held under control. Brutal syncopations knock the music off course; attempts to introduce sentiment are roughly dashed aside; a strange urgency imbues the movement with a character that the relative scarcity of notes hardly suggests on the printed page. Strangest of all is the central section, a whole series of rapid descending figures, each of which begins with a violent accent at the top of the keyboard and then, unexpectedly, slithers down hastily but quietly. It is like a climber perched on a cliff-face clutching desperately at a handhold that is almost out of reach; each time, the strain is more than exhausted fingertips can manage, and he slides a little further towards the fatal drop. The left hand, precarious in rhythm, does nothing to steady the music; it is a disturbing symbol of impotence, and being impotent, it dies away to nothingness.

Bowing to convention, Beethoven re-starts the movement, even allowing himself the luxury of a *ritenuto* on one dying fall; but again, the moment of pathos is shouted down. We are all ready for a violent ending, Beethoven seeming to be in his most unforgiving mood. But even this angry music is made to disintegrate; the movement ends with a curious collapse, the isolated chords all off the beat save for the final one, which brings an unexpected softness as it turns into the major. It is another symptom of Beethoven's wish to impose unity on the whole sonata; the traditionally clear-cut barriers between the movements are replaced by something much less defined. The scherzo emerges almost stealthily from the first movement, and then dissolves into the third. It is hardly a movement in its own right any more, but a fleeting episode that is over before we have fully adjusted to its premptory and abrupt demand.

We now stand on the threshold of the most revealing piece that Beethoven ever wrote. The first movement might be described as the apotheosis of classicism. Its beauties are gentle and lyrical, but they also have a sense of serene detachment—Olympian would be a misleading word, suggesting a more grandiose concept, yet there is something of Pallas Athene in its still, calm beauty. Like the Fourth Piano Concerto, it makes its mark by reticence; it is the music of a poet rather than a warrior. The scherzo impatiently brushes these abstractions aside, sparing little time for pleasantries; like most revolutions, it finds it easier to destroy than to rebuild, though its final bars acknowledge its impotence. Here is a situation then in which the classical concept has achieved perfection, which, in more cynical terms, is a way of saying 'a dead end'. Perfection cannot be surpassed. The scherzo lets in the 'Red Guards', but all they can do is to wreak havoc. Beethoven now turns his eyes inward, and in doing so, unbares his soul to us.

It takes courage for a performer to treat music with a proper mixture of authority and freedom. One must of course try to be true to the text, but that is only a beginning; what is also needed is a personal touch, though not so personal as to become eccentric or perverse. There can be few passages in the whole of Beethoven's compositions in which there are more detailed instructions than he now gives us. There is a paradox here since, in essence, what he is asking for is an abnormal freedom from conventional restraint; by giving us such an unusual number of exhortations, he tends to make us try to be even more punctilious than usual in observing them, and this can be an inhibiting factor. One must realize then that these are not rigid demarcations, but indications of flexibility of the most sensitive kind. Just to show how liberally the page has been scattered with *words* as opposed to notes, here is a reduction to chart form.

Bar 1. Adagio, ma non troppo. Una corda.

Bar 4. Recitativo. Piu adagio. Andante. Cresc.

Bar 5. Adagio. Sempre tenuto. Tutte le corde. Dimin. Ritardando. Cantabile. Una corda.

Bar 6. Meno adagio. Cresc. Adagio. ten. dimin. smorzando.

Bar 7. Adagio, ma non troppo. *p.* tutte le corde.

Bar 8. Cresc. Dim.

Bar 9. (Klagender gesang) Arioso dolente. *p.*

In the space of nine bars, Beethoven uses no less than forty-four
words or abbreviations, which must be something of a record;
this alone should be evidence that something exceptional is
taking place. Because the music has now become so intensely
personal, it matters far more to him that he should not be misunderstood. In the early days, one indication of tempo would
be enough for a whole movement because the music spoke for
itself (i.e. it was based on the Classical concept). Here, the indications are far more numerous because it speaks for *him*—the
hallmark of Romanticism by my definition.[1] The passage is so
unique that I quote it in full.

Ex. 120

[1] See p. 61.

The earliest anticipation of this degree of freedom in his piano music is to be found in the first movement of Op. 31 No. 2 in D minor. There too, Beethoven has several changes of tempo, even more marked in contrast, as well as recitative passages which have a very vocal quality about them.

Ex. 121

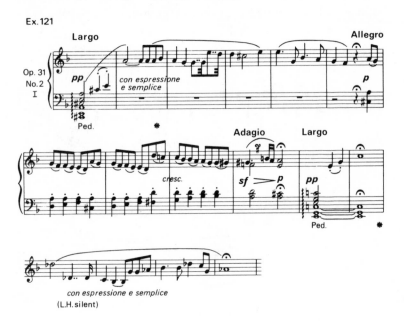

But profound though their effect may be, these are simply alternating sections of widely contrasted material, for which precedents may be discovered in innumerable compositions of the seventeenth and eighteenth centuries. What is so very different in the Op. 110 example is the enormous effort Beethoven has made to convey considerable freedom of tempo within a basically slow passage. He is demanding a flexibility that must seem to be spontaneous, a refinement of interpretation that musical notation has always been ill-equipped to indicate.

As to the repeated As (Ex. 120, bar 5), I shall not add to the enormous amount of speculation that has already been put down on paper as to precisely what Beethoven meant. As long as the effect is deeply expressive, I think it is perfectly acceptable to treat the passage freely, even to the extent of playing a few more notes if one feels moved to do so.

Once Beethoven has opened the door to his inner self, which I believe is the true function of Ex. 120, he reveals a profound grief, the more touching for its lack of rhetoric. The slow, pulsating harmonies are for the most part simple, only occasionally tinged with dissonance. One feels, without blasphemy, that here truly was 'a man of sorrows, acquainted with grief'. Not only was he acquainted with grief; he had become reconciled to it, and if there is one lesson to be learned from the late works of Beethoven it is that those passages that seem most violent in protest are railing, not against any personal despair, but against the inadequacy of his musical resources. It was the conflict with the material that he found so frustrating; the inner grief he could cope with, since it could be sublimated into musical terms. This brief *arioso*[1] is a perfect instance of such a sublimation. It ends with a gesture which, while in no way denying grief, seems to accept it without a trace of bitterness.

Ex.122

(L.H. in unison octaves)

---

[1] The melody is a more straightforward version of Ex. 126.

Beethoven's religious beliefs veered towards what we would think of as Humanism, although at times he was willing to accept orthodoxy. He was familiar with Eastern mysticism, and kept framed on his desk a significant phrase that he had copied out in his own hand.

I am that which is. I am all that was, that is, and that shall be.

Where a truly religious person would turn to the Bible for consolation in time of sorrow, I think it more probable that Beethoven would have looked for solace in music itself. I suspect that in his eyes, music was an aspect of divinity, an aspect he could comprehend more readily than anything the Church could offer. I do not think it too far-fetched, then, to suggest that at the end of the *arioso*, having exposed almost too openly his innermost feelings, he should seek consolation in the purest musical form, the fugue. It is as though he were to say to himself, 'This delving within hurts too much; let me return to the impersonal, detached world of classicism.' For subject, he chooses a pattern of such purity and serenity that it might have been carved in marble.

Ex.123

This grave and beautiful theme is a distillation of the essence of the very opening phrase of the sonata. Omit the first note of Ex. 111, and we find the melody consists of rising steps, Ab—Db—Bb—Eb ; this pattern has not only been the sole content of the development section, but has also been hinted at in Ex. 118— the first time that Beethoven plants the idea of reducing the theme to a succession of rising fourths. (You can see it in the lower part of the right hand.) The mere fact that it now eschews the sensuous garments of harmony is a symbol of purification. Moreover, the fugue is notable for its control. For the greater part, it is quiet and restrained; any tendency towards loudness is soon suppressed.

There is one fascinating moment which is worth mentioning, although I willingly admit that my interpretation is open to challenge. The first time that Beethoven admits a *f* into the texture is at the fourth entry of the subject.

Ex.124

Now Beethoven is being at his most pedantic in matters of notation here, as the awkwardness of the 'tails-up and tails-down' in the right hand shows. He is determined to keep the counterpoint absolutely clear. The point that intrigues me, though, stems from the duplication of the mark *f* in *both* hands in the first bar of Ex. 124.[1] It lasts for these four bars only, and then the indication *diminuendo* brings us back to a long continuation, all kept at a low level of sound. When at last a crescendo does begin, it too dissolves rapidly, the music being reduced to two slender lines of counterpoint in the right hand. Then comes the moment that intrigues me so, a massive entry of the fugue subject in octaves, touched with additional drama by being put in the minor for the first time.

Ex.125

---

[1] See *Ur-text*, published by Henle.

The conventional view is to regard this bass entry as the sort of thing that happens so often in a Bach organ fugue, the subject appearing on the pedals with majestic effect. A close look at the copy reveals a possibly significant difference between this and the earlier octave entry of Ex. 124. There, as I pointed out, Beethoven took the trouble to write *f* in both hands; here there is only the one *ff*, which directly contradicts the *p* of the preceding bar. We have seen how Mozart can employ conflicts between *f* and *p* in Ex. 27. There is no reason therefore why Beethoven should not do the same thing, and for the same reason—to contrast the frailty of the right-hand part with the strength of the bass. If this reading is correct (and I personally am very drawn to it), it gives an extraordinary quality to this moment, as though the 'temple' were being rocked by an earthquake. It is not long before the fugue recedes into its initial calm. Soon, a final crescendo leads us to what appears to be a triumphant conclusion. But no; at the very moment when victory seems to be in our grasp, the music loses all confidence, comes to a halt on a chord that is far from final, and then sinks despondently back into the minor key. Could disillusionment be more graphically expressed? It is the cry of despair; the hoped-for consolation has failed to materialize, and he must sink even deeper into the abyss. Once again the haunting theme of the *arioso* returns, this time broken by little silences that give an increased pathos to an already grief-stricken melody.

Ex.126

The music disintegrates, the pattern of Ex. 122 being repeated, but with each note now isolated from its neighbours. There follows one of the strangest passages Beethoven ever wrote, the chord of G major repeated no fewer than ten times, constantly growing in intensity, but always preserving this sense of isolation. The silences outnumber the chords; they are like great gulping breaths, the gasps of a dying man. I find this passage very near to Berlioz in spirit, in its combination of a rather naïve imagery with an intensely dramatic idea. Naturally, there are other ways of interpreting it, but none that accounts for its unique effect quite so convincingly.

At this, the darkest hour of all, what can Beethoven do but again seek for consolation in the purest form of music? He returns to the fugue in an even more cerebral form, the subject inverted, the shape seen as in a mirror.

Ex.127

(p)

There are times in a man's life when work is one of the only cures for some great personal grief—the loss of a dearly loved one, the collapse of some cherished hope. The sheer self-discipline involved is a salutary corrective to self-pity; so now, I feel, does Beethoven brace himself with still more intellectual a challenge. The result is little short of miraculous, for in due course, as we shall see, the theme is transformed.

Imagine a great dam containing a vast reservoir; as we watch, small trickles of water begin to percolate between the huge stones that make up the face of the dam. Even after the first dislodgements, the great arc still stays in place, but as the trickles become a torrent, the weight of water suddenly overwhelms us, sweeping everything away from its path. In my analogy, the dam is the inherent restraint of Classicism, the water is the emotional tide of Romanticism. Seen in these terms, this passage, symbolizing the ultimate collapse of an entire musical era, is awe-inspiring.

The first cracks in the facade appear with this phrase:

Ex.128

the fact that this is what is called a diminution of the subject (i.e. the theme of the fugue quickened) lends weight to my theory that Beethoven is becoming more and more intellectual, trying to contain the inner force by every means in his power. Simultaneously with these disruptive phrases, we also find the fugue subject in augmentation, notes twice as slow.

Ex.129

The rhythm grows more and more chaotic, so that all continuity of pulse is destroyed; for some few bars, every single first beat is suppressed, as though the very foundations were being swept away.

At this point, Beethoven has a tricky problem of notation. He wants the music to be gaining in impetus the whole time—he has even asked for that in words; but as the trickle increases to a flood, as more and more notes crowd into a bar, the actual pulse must be slowed to accommodate them. He therefore says, 'Meno Allegro' or 'less quickly' at the very point that the music sounds as though it is growing quicker. It is the exact equivalent of a change of gear.

Ex.130

'Chaos..'   'change of gear'

Although it is my belief that this movement is the perfect

symbol of the Revolution that Beethoven accomplished, it can easily be seen that it is being brought about in an entirely Evolutionary manner. The pattern at this 'Meno Allegro' may look very different from the serene fugue subject, but it is so closely related as to be virtually identical. Only two notes have been omitted (xx).

Ex.131

As if to emphasize the essential continuity of the music, Beethoven manages to keep the fugue subject going in one way or another. Even the inverted form of Ex. 127 reappears, distorted it is true by the flying pieces of fugal material that seem almost to be attacking it, but still there.

Ex.132

After all the turbulence, the safe haven of A♭ major is reached at last, and the fugue subject boldly reappears in the bass, free of distortion.

We now come to the crux of the matter, on which my entire view of this sonata must stand or fall. Naturally, every previous analysis of this work has pointed out the triumphant emergence of the fugue subject; some go so far as to use some such phrase as 'the fugue subject transformed'. This seems to me to miss the point completely. Suppose that only one page of this sonata had been preserved, the last page; suppose even that we had no more than these few bars:

Ex.133

ten thousand scholars could look at that through microscopes for a decade, and not one of them would be so foolish as to suggest it might be part of a fugue. There is nothing remotely 'fugal' about the writing; fugues are contrapuntal, and there is no counterpoint here, only a striding melody over a turbulent accompaniment. It is not the triumphant emergence of the fugue subject; it is the triumphant emergence of a *rhapsody*. The shackles of classicism have been severed; the new freedom is embraced with fervour, just as surely as in the ninth symphony, Beethoven rejects the material of the first three movements, saying 'Not with these tones...' and welcomes something completely new.

Compare the ending of this sonata with the closing pages of the mighty fugue that is the culmination of the Brahms–Handel Variations, and you will see at once what I mean. Even though Brahms introduces massive chords, the music remains essentially fugal in character. The whole point of Op. 110 seems to me that only by pushing beyond the limitations of classical form (as represented by the fugue) does Beethoven find the release from suffering that he has searched for for so long. That this release happens to contain the same elements as the previous music is a glorious affirmation that the solution to man's problems lies within himself.

CHAPTER IX

A WORD ON CRITICISM

THE VIEWPOINT put forward in the previous chapter is a very personal one, supported by an intuitive approach to the notes themselves rather than by any documentary evidence. It is, I hope, nearer the mark than the critic who wrote on 11 September 1806:

> Recently there was given the overture to Beethoven's opera, 'Fidelio', and all impartial musicians and music lovers were in perfect agreement that never was anything as incoherent, shrill, chaotic, and ear-splitting produced in music. The most piercing dissonances clash in a really atrocious harmony, and a few puny ideas only increase the disagreeable and deafening effect.[1]

Nor can I agree with a contemporary verdict on his Second Symphony, which described it as 'a crass monster, a hideously wounded dragon that refuses to expire, and, though bleeding in the finale, furiously beats about with its tail erect'.[1] All the same, there is something of value in these reactions, grotesque though they may seem to us today. We may think of the Moonlight sonata as a Beautiful Work, but Beethoven certainly wanted us to be electrified by the finale. Suppose that I had been a reasonably conservative listener in Beethoven's time, and had been given the job of writing a criticism of Op. 27 No. 2 in C♯ minor for a daily paper. Following the examples I have just quoted, I suspect that I could have written something like this.

> Herr Beethoven's latest composition reverses all expectation by commencing with an *adagio*, a procedure which is scarcely

[1] Both quotations are culled from Nicholas Slonimsky: *Lexicon of Musical Invective*: Coleman-Ross, 1953.

121

to be recommended since it revealed a total lack of contrast in ideas, and none of the considered musical argument which we have come to expect as proper in a work dignified by the name of Sonata. The monotonous repetition of triplets throughout the entire movement, some of them revealing almost laughable faults in harmony, could only produce a feeling of *ennui* in the listener. The second movement was a pleasing enough trifle, though somewhat too brief to make any lasting effect. As for the finale, it proved to be an hysterical jangling of notes which was impossible to grasp at a single hearing, nor was it likely to encourage one to undergo the experience a second time. If Herr Beethoven can do no better than to assault the keyboard in this brutal manner, he would be advised to apprentice himself to a blacksmith, preferably an harmonious one.

I would like at this point to suggest a paradox. Although such a hypothetical criticism strikes us as outrageous today, it is right in a way. The reaction seems all wrong, and yet it is nearer to the truth, nearer even to what Beethoven sub-consciously wanted, than our own tendency to sit back and wallow in the beauties of an accepted masterpiece. It merely draws the wrong conclusions from the evidence. In fact, we *ought* to be aware of the monotony of the triplets in the first movement, not as a means of producing *ennui*, but as a deliberate calculation on Beethoven's part. He knows that we are expecting contrast, so he witholds it. We should be aware of the alleged 'faults' in the harmony, for they are Beethoven's way of expressing pain, of giving profundity to a movement that might otherwise have been merely pretty. We should notice the economy and reticence of the second movement, and we should certainly respond to the terrifying impact of the finale, which is not a series of clearly articulated arpeggios from a primer on piano technique, but the musical equivalent of a volcano in eruption.

Now to watch a volcano on film is an awe-inspiring and thrilling sight; to run from it as it destroys your home is a nightmare. It is part of the creative artist's job to enable us to experience emotions at every level. As total human beings we may expect to find occasional moments of exaltation, a reasonable portion of happiness, a fair amount of boredom, stabs of pain—physical and emotional—and deep troughs of despair. They come to us all in varying degrees, even though we may not have the artist's ability to crystallize them and translate them into a durable form. A great sonata is like a life compressed; in it we may find the emotion of a lifetime, although obviously not in any chronological order. But what of quality; how do we recognize greatness and what is it?

Relatively, the grief of a seven-year-old child when its adored puppy is run over is as great as the heartbreak of a woman whose lover is killed in a war. The child recovers more quickly because, however sharp the pain at the time, it doesn't actually go so deep. There is a similarity in music. A third-rate composer can simulate grief perfectly well, but in the long run, it is only the grief of a seven-year-old. Beethoven's pain was the pain of an adult, an adult moreover who had suffered so much that he was able to transcend the personal and become universal. It is the Christian belief that Christ carries the burden of our sins; I do not consider it blasphemous to say that Bach, Mozart and Beethoven carry the burden of our sorrows. I certainly feel so when I hear or play something like the *Arioso* from Op. 110.

What is hard to accept is that for all its emotional profundity, there is not one note, not one chord, that has not been precisely chosen by Beethoven. The music seems to speak spontaneously, and yet it is full of artifice. How conscientiously he writes down every smallest rest, the calculated gaps in the melodic line that are like suppressed tears, the disturbing elements in the harmony that are like a stab of pain. To imagine that this emotion that Beethoven shares with us is not harnessed throughout by intellectual control is to be completely deluded about the true nature of composition. But we do not need to be consciously aware of what a cynic might call the 'tricks of the trade' to respond to the emotion, because by now the language of Beethoven has become sufficiently familiar for us to be able to get the message, even though we may not appreciate the subtlety or daring with which it is expressed. The composer himself uses craftsmanship in varying degrees, sometimes taking intuitive short-cuts, sometimes labouring mightily, sometimes falling back on sheer technical expertise.

I am not suggesting for one moment that Beethoven was consciously aware of the sort of scenario I have suggested for Op. 110. I believe my interpretation of the evidence is valid, or I would not have put it forward; but it is only valid in the light of our knowledge of the whole corpus of Beethoven's work, and of what came afterwards. (Even so, there is some confirmation in his treatment of the finale of the ninth symphony, as I have already pointed out.)

My real reason for including this short essay is to draw attention to the danger attendant on familiarity. It is said to breed contempt, though I cannot believe that anybody who professes contempt for Beethoven has the remotest claim to familiarity with his works. There is a risk, however, that we may come to take them for granted, paying lip-service to their greatness, while secretly feeling that their impact has become somewhat dulled. It is here that my view of a constantly evolving language can help to preserve the freshness that these works had when first we heard them, for the simple reason that we cannot have heard them all at once. When our knowledge of Beethoven is wide enough to be able to trace a link, however tenuous, between the first and last sonatas, using the Appassionata as the central point, we find an added interest in every work. We see the man developing as we might watch one of our own family develop. Few composers have exciting lives; they are too busy writing notes on paper to have time for adventures. They live through their music, and music is a magical time machine that enables us to share their triumphs and disasters in astonishingly vivid terms. By all means let us search for the heart of the matter, but not if it means that our own hearts cease to be involved. Better to hate Beethoven than to remain aloof . . .

CHAPTER X

SCHUBERT

The last great trilogy

Sonata in C minor. D.958.
1. Allegro. 2. Adagio. 3. Menuetto. 4. Allegro.

Sonata in A major. D. 959.
1. Allegro. 2. Adantino. 3. Scherzo: Allegro vivace. 4. Rondo: Allegretto.

Sonata in B♭ major. D.960.
1. Molto Moderato. 2. Andante sostenuto. 3. Scherzo: Allegro vivace con delicatezza. 4. Allegro ma non troppo.

First published by Diabelli in 1838, in an edition dedicated (by the publisher) to Schumann. Schubert had intended to dedicate the three sonatas to Hummel; but as Hummel died in 1837, Diabelli, always an opportunist, decided to change the dedication.

B Y N O W, it is fairly general knowledge that Mozart wrote his last three symphonies in one extraordinary creative outburst of six or seven weeks; another equally remarkable achievement has not been mentioned so frequently. In September 1828, Schubert, who had received nothing like as much acclaim as Mozart during his lifetime, wrote three massive sonatas for piano whose total length must exceed the duration of Mozart's three final symphonies by a substantial margin. I realize that this in itself is not necessarily a significant yardstick; we do not measure music by the foot or the minute, nor are long works automatically better than short ones. But Schubert's last three sonatas, which he specifically labelled 'Drei grosse Sonaten', are to his total compositions for piano what Opp. 109, 110 and 111 are to Beethoven's. If the comparison is not wholly fair, it is because Schubert was able to learn a great deal more from Beethoven than Beethoven could from his predecessors. Although Haydn, Mozart and even lesser figures like Clementi unquestionably contributed a good deal to Beethoven as a young man, he was to move increasingly into a world of his own. Schubert, who outlived Beethoven only by a year and a half,[1] was able to benefit from his example. Not having any pretensions to being a concert pianist himself,[2] it is impossible for us to judge how well Schubert knew the Beethoven sonatas in terms of actual playing. Did he, as one would expect, read them through at the keyboard whenever he could obtain copies? Could he even afford to buy them? Certainly he revered Beethoven above all other composers, and, in his humility, would have felt that to be interred next to his idol was an honour he could never deserve. Those loving friends who saw to it that he was buried in an adjacent grave were paying him the greatest compliment they could. It was an ironic one, for Schubert had found all too little fame in his lifetime, except in his successful partnership with the singer Vogl. An English musical dictionary published in 1827 devotes more space to Beethoven than to any other composer of the time; Schubert is not even mentioned, so little was the outside world aware of his genius.

Two men could hardly ever have worked more differently at the same craft; Beethoven's melodies were often the result of months, even years, of patient endeavour, changing a rhythm here, an interval there, beginning sometimes from commonplace banalities that one is surprised to find him even bothering to write down. Schubert had so natural a melodic gift that he could write as many as three complete songs in a day; his 'sketches' of a movement are often little less than a hastily scribbled rough copy in which it is clear from the handwriting that his pen could

[1] Beethoven: 1770–1827. Schubert: 1797–1828.
[2] Mozart, Beethoven, Chopin, Liszt, Brahms, Rachmaninoff, Bartók—to name only a few—were all successful as concert players.

scarcely keep up with his thoughts. When one speaks of his prodigious facility, it was not of an academic, trained kind, such as we find in Mozart, Haydn or Bach. The contrapuntal feats that astonish us in Bach's Musical Offering or in the finale of the Jupiter symphony do not come naturally; they are a sort of musical sleight-of-hand, acquired by years of practice, and by having what one might term a musical crossword-puzzle mentality. The fact that the crosswords happen also to be poetry is one of the miracles of music. Schubert's facility was more horizontal than vertical, by which I mean that his first impulse was to travel across the page in pursuit of a melody; some of his most inspired twists of harmony have an almost accidental air to them, and I tend to think that they were indeed happy discoveries of the moment rather than carefully planned.

Not even his most ardent admirer would seriously maintain that the complete piano sonatas of Schubert are as significant a contribution to the literature of the piano as those of Beethoven. It is no accident that the most played keyboard works of Schubert are the Impromptus, Moments Musicaux, the Wanderer Fantasy, and the F minor Fantasy for piano duet. Had he been born some twenty years later and grown up alongside Schumann and Chopin, I suspect that he might have written far fewer sonatas, and occupied himself with shorter forms to which his essentially lyrical gift was more suited. The overall perfection of the songs is something to marvel at; but with the example of Beethoven before him, he obviously felt a tremendous urge to write symphonies and sonatas. It was by accepting their challenge that he himself would be accepted. However beautiful the songs were, audiences of the time could scarcely estimate them as highly as we do today, since they could have realized neither the sheer magnitude of his achievement nor its historical importance. Here then is one of the ironies of musical history, a composer perfectly equipped by nature to write miniatures, drawn compulsively towards the very peaks which presented the greatest perils. Mahler and Schubert have much in common in this respect.

The use of the word 'miniature' may seem both derogatory

and provocative. Schubert's major works are far from concise; could a miniaturist conceive such compositions as the great C major symphony or the Octet, both of them immensely long, though unquestionable masterpieces? The answer obviously must be 'yes', or he would not have written them; but they are saved by the virtue of the unteachable qualities of genius. Sonata form was not the natural medium for Schubert to use; for instance, when he was still young he devised what seems at first glance to be a highly ingenious approach to the Recapitulation. Instead of beginning again in the tonic key, he would start in what is called the sub-dominant, the key a fifth lower. While this gives a deceptive air of surprise to the re-entry of the first subject, it is actually a lazy short-cut, as this little plan reveals.

NORMAL FORM	SCHUBERT'S DEVICE
Exposition	
Ist subject. TONIC. Bridge modulates to 2nd subject. DOMINANT	Ist subject. TONIC. Bridge modulates to 2nd subject. DOMINANT
Recapitulation	
Ist subject. TONIC. Bridge modified to stay in TONIC for 2nd subject (i.e. different from Exposition)	Ist subject. SUB-DOMINANT. Bridge does identical modulation up a 5th which brings us back to TONIC for 2nd subject (i.e. same as Exposition)

In other words, all Schubert had to do when he got to the start of his recapitulation was to copy his exposition exactly, merely transposing the first subject down a fifth. It's a clever idea, but it defeats the dramatic function of the Recapitulation and minimizes the necessity for any new invention. It is evidence that he misunderstood the true function of the form. Later, when he acquired a maturer view, he was to make a much more important contribution; having a remarkable flair for modulation into unexpected and remote keys, he decided to break the unwritten law that second subjects must always be in the dominant (or the relative major if the sonata happened to be in a minor key). With the complete conviction that only true genius can bring to unorthodoxy, he would introduce his second subject material in a totally foreign key. This was true invention, whereas his earlier device had been little more than an ingenious trick.

In the last year of his life, the year of these sonatas, Schubert must have become aware of some deficiences in his technical equipment; he even tried to take a formal course of counterpoint with a renowned teacher called Sechter. Death deprived him of the chance, but his several attempts at writing fugues show that he was very much in earnest. A great deal of his music existed in a vacuum; he never heard any of his mature orchestral music for the simple reason that it was not performed in his lifetime. The first five symphonies were written by the time that he was eighteen; as Donald Tovey has pointed out with devastating logic, 'Every work Schubert left us is an early work'. Had Beethoven died at the same age, he would have written only one symphony, three piano concertos, the Op. 18 set of quartets and the first fifteen piano sonatas (up to Op. 28). Seen in this perspective, whose achievement was the greater?

Let us turn to the subject in hand. There is no doubt that Schubert intended these last three piano sonatas to be a trilogy, since they are numbered 1, 2 and 3 in his own hand. I marvel that even Schubert, with all his facility, was able to compose the three works in one month. Yet, when we look at them closely, there are quite a few points of resemblance between them, as though the ideas that were churning round in his mind had become so enmeshed with each other that try as he might, he could not disentangle them. Is there perhaps a more subtle explanation? Did Schubert envisage deliberate links between the three works, so that they would in effect become one gigantic sonata, each 'movement' of which was a complete sonata in itself? I don't want to labour the point, and indeed it may not be worth making; but once I had realized that the three sonatas were written in so short a period, my attitude towards them changed. Similarities between the openings of the first two sonatas, between the finales of the first and third, between the slow movements of the second and third, and even more notably between the beautiful coda to the first movement of No. 2 and the still more beautiful coda to the slow movement of No. 3, begin to add up to something more than just coincidence. The similarities of construction are probably less significant, since each one might be said to be typical of Schubert's way of manipulating the form.

I have already suggested that Schubert was drawn towards writing sonatas because of his admiration for Beethoven. This is particularly apparent in the first sonata of this unique trilogy, the one in C minor. It begins with a theme of immense power, its massive quality partly derived from the fact that the bass stays solidly rooted on the tonic for so long, while the melody reaches out further and further from the starting point.

Ex.134

Now it is impossible not to be aware of the very close resemblance between this theme and the one with which Beethoven begins his thirty-two Variations in C minor. No doubt the tribute was unconscious, but it underlines Schubert's assumption of a Beethoven posture, to say the least.

Ex.135

* Legend has it that years after writing these variations, Beethoven heard them being practised by a girl student. Failing to recognize the work, he asked who had composed it; on being told it was his own, he expressed dismay, saying, 'Such nonsense by me? O Beethoven, what an ass you were!'

Was Brahms also tapping the same source when he conceived the mighty Passacaglia that comprises the last movement of his Fourth Symphony?

Ex. 136

* Try a G♯ here and the resemblance becomes more striking.

The greater richness of harmony reflects the age in which Brahms lived, but there can be no doubting the similarity of musical intent that exists in these three examples. To place Schubert thus as a link between Beethoven and Brahms is only proper, since it would be fair to say that Brahms was even more influenced by Schubert than he was by Beethoven.

It is interesting that both Beethoven and Brahms used this framework as the basis for a massive set of variations. Schubert too is aware of the enormous possibilities such a strong harmonic sequence offers. After a couple of descending scales that also recall moments in Beethoven (the finale of the Pathétique and the first movement of Op. 90), he sets out on a direct variation of Ex. 134.

Ex. 137

Such discipline proved foreign to his temperament however, and this is as far as he can go without launching into a new, lyrical extension. The song-writer takes over from the musical architect, and the dramatic tension goes out of the movement. This struggle between the two aspects of Schubert's personality is fascinating to watch; his aspirations are so frequently at odds with his inclinations. He is certainly aware of the hazards involved; the second subject, full of felicities of harmony, is lovingly explored at some length. Then, as if to prove his ability to accept the intellectual challenge of sonata form, he subjects it to a rigorous treatment, putting it into the minor and disguising its gentle outline with rather choppy figuration.

The development is remarkable. At first hearing, it seems to have little to do with the exposition, and one is tempted to dismiss it as irrelevant rambling, touched with inspiration it is true, but lacking the compactness of argument we have come to expect in a sonata. In fact, it is an admirable example of Schubert's inventive genius. Rambling is scarcely the right word to describe music that occupies itself entirely with one idea for a page and a half. What worries us is that the idea seems to have no relationship to what has gone before. Here is this new theme he seems to be so taken with (Ex. 138):

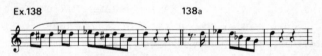

Its most noticeable feature is the 'narrowness' of the intervals. Now the opening theme, Ex. 134, is also concerned with narrow intervals; its culmination (not quoted in Ex. 134) is a pattern which I have shown, conveniently transposed, in Ex. 138a. Marry elements of Ex. 137 and 138a, and one can begin to see that Ex. 138 is far from irrelevant. It is not so much a development of a theme as its 'descendant'. Here then is the clue that shows us that Schubert was far from incompetent in his handling of large forms. We will find the same technique being employed in all three sonatas; it is a precursor of that 'transformation' of themes which was to became the favourite practice of composers such as Berlioz, Liszt and Tchaikovsky. In Schubert's hands, the device is used less obviously; but once we see how subtly he uses what might be called a process of melodic evolution, passages that seemed diffuse and irrelevant are seen to be very much to the point.

I have already touched on the similarities that exist between these sonatas. Even though there is a world of difference between the mood of the C minor sonata and its successor in A major, the rhythmic resemblance is strong. Compare bars 4–6 of Ex. 134 with this next example and you will see what I mean.

Ex.139

Similarities of modulation are easier to sense than to demonstrate. Here, for instance, is a quite remarkable passage from the finale of the C minor sonata. It shows Schubert at his most ingenious; if, to our ears, he seems to indulge in a sequence too many, we must remember how fantastically swift the changes of key must have seemed to a listener in 1828; it takes time to take in the formula that the composer has devised.

Ex.140

If we turn to the thirty-second bar of the A major sonata, we find a sequence which is nearly as unusual. The constitution of the harmonies is curiously similar, and if we merely change the rhythm to the characteristic ♩ ♪♩ ♪ of the previous example, the resemblance becomes much clearer.

Ex.141

(D. 959. I)

Another instance of this sort of cross-fertilization of harmony can be traced from the A major sonata to the glorious B♭ sonata which follows it. Since we are concerned with harmony, I will reduce the music to its fundamentals. Notice that in the first example, from D.959, the 'shift' note in the harmony is to be found at the top; in D.960, the 'shift' note is at first in the bass, but the technique is so similar that one passage seems to be a mirror of the other.

Ex.142

(D. 959. I)

Ex.142a

(D. 960. I)

★ Also, see Ex. 162.

At the end of the first movement of D.959, the A major sonata, Schubert has a coda of extraordinary beauty; for the first and only time, the proud opening subject (which he has completely neglected during the development) is seen as though from afar, wrapped in a romantic haze that changes its entire character. This, coupled with some modulations that only he could have conceived, provides us with one of the most memorable phrases in the whole movement.

Ex.143

(D.959.I)

The effect of the delicately placed bass-notes, like a softly plucked 'cello, is unforgettable; the writing breathes a serenity that few other composers could ever achieve. Yet if we turn to the slow movement of the B♭ sonata, D.960, we find a passage that not only excels this in sheer beauty, but seems to be derived directly from it. If I change Schubert's notation by doubling the note-values—it need not affect the sound at all—the likeness is easier to see with the eye.

Ex.144

(D. 960)

The textures are virtually identical. The later sonata shows a rather more complex treatment, but that is only to be expected, since it is the main substance of the movement and not the inspired afterthought that it seems to be in D.959.

The sublime melody of the slow movement of D.960 appears complete in every detail in Schubert's 'rough' sketch; but the central section of the movement was recast entirely. He hit upon a fairly close approximation to the final version, but laid it out so that the contrasting theme in A major was given to the left hand.

Ex.145

The accompanying figure in the right hand was a little too fussy, and for all his haste in committing these sonatas to paper, Schubert had enough critical faculty to be able to make an extensive revision of this section. The version we now know has a far greater nobility than his first draft.

Mention of his critical faculty leads me to a fascinating demonstration of how a composer can have second thoughts. The finale of the A major sonata is a Rondo, based on a theme of immediate appeal.

Ex.146

(D. 959. IV)

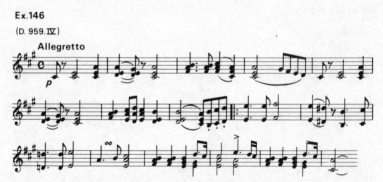

A version of this tune appears in far more than embryonic form in an earlier sonata (D.537) written in March 1817. Schubert presumably felt that anything more than ten years old must already have been consigned to oblivion. He therefore resuscitated the melody, altering it as he saw fit, not, I am convinced, to disguise it, but to show what experience could teach. Here now is the earlier version, and a close comparison of the two is instructive. (The tune is in octaves throughout.)

Ex.147

(D. 537. II)

Allegretto quasi andantino

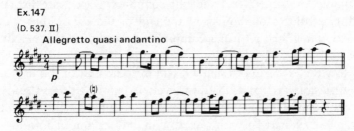

Both are beguiling, but there is no doubt that the later version (Ex. 146) shows a far greater awareness of craftsmanship.

The B♭ Sonata, one of the supreme masterpieces of the whole piano literature, is the one in which Schubert most successfully comes to terms with his own natural genius. It is almost as though he had said, 'Why must I try to measure my strength against Beethoven; let me be content to be myself'. Since his instinct drew him most readily to song, the sonata is the most lyrical ever written. To cavil at its length is to show a churlish ingratitude, for even Schubert was never more generous with melody than he is here. Over an accompaniment of remarkable simplicity, he extends a first subject whose serene character is enhanced by its tendency to move step by step, with the minimum of wide intervals.

Ex.148

(D. 960. I)

Molto moderato

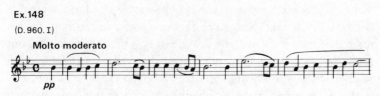

There follows a touch which instantly gives the stamp of romanticism to this otherwise rather classical melody, a low, distant trill that might well have been suggested by thunder heard far away in the mountains on a fine autumn day. There is a silence, as though the contemplation of a perfect landscape had indeed been momentarily disturbed; then, unaffected by the remote possibility of storms ahead, the song continues. Once more there is a distant rumble of thunder at the end of the phrase, but it is quickly integrated into an accompanying figure, and the melody goes on its way.

Now the problem of using a broad melodic span of this nature as a first subject is that it is hard to develop something that is already so complete. The very word 'develop' presupposes the idea of extension, of starting with a small unit, and causing it to grow. For instance, if I were to take the notes B♭—A—B♭ which appear in the first bar of Ex. 148, I could 'develop' them in the classical sense of the word, by doing something on these lines.

Ex.149

If the result of this little exercise has been to fuse elements from the finale of Mozart's Jupiter symphony with a significant theme from the opening bar of Brahms' second symphony, it is hardly surprising. Fragments such as this are the stock material of the composer bent on development; they are readily manipulated, flexible, and easy to recognize in disguised forms.[1] For Schubert to develop his melody in this way would inevitably mean sacrificing its very essence—the long line as opposed to the concise rhythm. No sonata that I have discussed so far in this book has so long an opening theme; the nearest to it is the Appassionata, but there, as we have seen, the purpose of the theme is fundamentally to suggest the *harmony* of F minor. Beethoven's Op. 110 also begins with an extended melody, but it falls into two clearly defined sections. Schubert's mature genius shows itself in his solution to the

[1] For a detailed analysis of Brahms' treatment of this very theme, see *Talking about Symphonies*, Chapter VII, pp. 109–15.

problem; instead of developing by the accumulation of fragments, he develops by modifying the shape of the initial tune. The starting-note, B♭, becomes the third note of the scale of G♭ major, a beautifully subtle twist which at once opens up new possibilities.

Ex.150

Here we have the hand of a master at work. The drift from melodic to harmonic thinking is barely perceptible. The four notes in the fifth bar bring the first suggestion of a chord as opposed to a line of melody; they are repeated two bars later, and then we are gently rocked into harmonic motion. There is none of the abruptness with which Beethoven changes the texture in Op. 110 (see Ex. 112); yet the function of the two passages is identical insofar as they lead us from an essentially song-like concept to a purely instrumental one. At the very moment when it seems as though things may be getting out of hand, Schubert restores order by bringing back the opening theme. It is the first *forte* of the movement.

As is so often the case, it is instructive to consider an alternative. Musical scholars have sometimes led us to believe that Schubert lacked discipline in composition, that he worked 'off the cuff' to such a degree that he was too easily led away from the matter in hand. It is an argument that has some substance, but in this sonata we are dealing not with the inspired ramblings of a teenage boy, but the work of a vastly experienced composer. By way of experiment, let us suppose that Schubert had got carried away by the excitement of these triplet chords. How easy it would have been to have digressed into something quite out of keeping with the movement as a whole.

Ex.151

Schubert avoids such temptations; he uses the first bar of Ex. 151 as a pivot that enables him to slide effortlessly back into the home key of B♭ major; the theme emerges triumphant, but subtly changed by the fact that it now rests on a sustained dominant in the base instead of the original tonic. It prevents us from having too strong a sense of finality; sure enough, there are surprises just ahead. With a modulation of typical daring, he flings us into the totally unexpected tonality of F♯ minor.

At first glance one is tempted to dismiss this as shock for shock's sake. A little thought shows us how carefully Schubert has prepared the ground—or perhaps it would be fairer to say how surely his musical instincts led him. For fourteen bars, starting from the beginning of Ex. 150, the music has clearly been in G♭ major. Now the notation of the scale of G♭ *minor* is extremely cumbersome, so it is habitually written as F♯ minor—the same sounds, but considerably easier to read or write.[1]

G♭ minor harmonic   F♯ minor

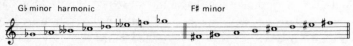

[1] A key-signature for G♭ minor is theoretically impossible, but it's an amusing academic exercise to invent one. It would look like this:

Small wonder that composers, publishers and musicians prefer the three sharps that suffice for F♯ minor.

The point of this excursion into the heady delights of musical theory is to show the justification for using F♯ minor as a key for the second subject of a sonata in B♭ major. By all precedent, the second subject should be in the dominant key of F major; but by dividing his first subject into two clear sections, one based on B♭, and the other based on G♭, Schubert has given us what feels like *two* tonics to choose from. To put his second subject into the minor version of this subsidiary tonic is an inspired way of getting the best of both worlds. The new key is wildly remote from the true tonic of B♭, but closely related to the subsidiary tonic, G♭.

Technical analysis of this type is as abhorrent to my nature as fugues were to Schubert's, but there are occasions when one has to show an awareness of the law, if only to reveal how cleverly it has been broken.

The second subject material is full of riches, showing the same process of melodic evolution that Schubert exploits so skilfully in the opening pages. There comes a point, however, when he seems in danger of drifting into the commonplace. Figures that have a vague suggestion of students' exercises in piano technique begin to monopolize the page.

Ex.152

In the hands of a great artist this can sound exquisite, but looked at dispassionately, it must be admitted to be something of a ready-made formula. How marvellous then that Schubert should have found ways of making such familiar devices peculiarly relevant to this sonata. The subconscious of a composer works in a mysterious way, and I am convinced that Schubert himself was unaware of what I am going to show you now; yet I am equally sure that it is a valid example of the instinctive sense of balance in matters of musical architecture which I have already commented upon in earlier chapters. Here first is a small part of the second subject material; it appears in two forms—first as simple chords, one to each beat, and then in this more active rhythm.

Ex.153

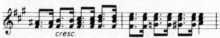

Now wouldn't it seem the most natural thing in the world to balance such a phrase with an answer that gave a hint of the pattern without actually being a true mirror?

Ex.154

Apply a few touches of make-up:

Ex.154a

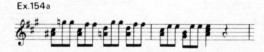

transpose into the key of the moment:

Ex.154b

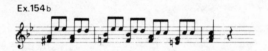

and you have precisely the sort of figure that soon emerges from the misleadingly pedantic triplets of Ex. 152. It bears a suggestion of melody, while recognizing that in a primarily melodic move-ment, the ear needs some contrast. It is different in texture from any of the preceding sections, and yet, as I have shown, seems to have a sense of 'rightness' that only comes with the sure touch of genius.

A new, even more delightful example of this sureness of touch is to be found in a moment. Schubert is heading for the safe haven of the dominant in order to be able to bring his exposition to a proper conclusion. He has a problem though which would have appealed to Lewis Carroll. One can imagine the perplexed voice of Alice saying 'But how do you arrive

at somewhere you're already *at*?'. I spoke of Schubert heading
for the haven of the dominant; the fact is that he has already
arrived there at the start of Ex. 152. How then can he give
us a feeling of arrival? His solution is brilliant. Like a conjurer
who seems to be making the most awful mess of a trick, Schubert
begins a series of abortive journeys into other keys, even stopping
and starting as if he had lost all sense of direction. The effect of this
is to disorientate our feeling of any tonal security. The changes
are so swift, so unexpected, that when we finally do arrive back at
F major, we have virtually forgotten what it sounded like.
Presented here in simplified form, we can follow the stages of this
diversion which, like those devised by urban highway authorities,
takes us into the back streets, getting us thoroughly lost before
we finally find our bearings again. (Imagine the figuration of
Ex. 154b throughout.)

Ex.155

Bar 1 seems to be heading straight for F major; bar 2 turns
us right away to Ab major in bar 3, which at once gives way
to Eb major in a half-hearted sort of way; bar 4, after a non-
plussed silence, starts in Gb major, only to slide into an equally
unconvincing Db major; a diminished seventh in bar 6 puts
us momentarily into no-man's-land while at the same time
suggesting the dominant of Bb; bar 7 seems to confirm that
maybe we are going to Bb after all; bar 8 says, 'Goodness, look
here we are in F'.

After so eventful a journey, we need time to settle down,
and Schubert unfolds a radiant new tune, richly harmonized.

Ex.156

Once again we can see Schubert's evolutionary process at work. The most notable feature of the second subject has been a tune beginning like this:

Ex.157

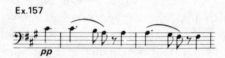

Each time it has appeared, there has been a note of wistfulness in the surrounding harmony; in a sense, the melody remains unfulfilled until it reaches the version we find in Ex. 156. While it is presumably correct in textbook terms to label Ex. 156 a 'codetta', it is considerably more enlightening to see it as the apotheosis of the second subject.

This sonata is immensely long, but its proportions are nobly realized. Schubert is very much aware of the danger of losing our attention at this juncture. We have reached the dominant; we have been offered a delectable morsel of melody; it is the moment to tantalize us a little more. He repeats Ex. 156 an octave lower, rich as divided violas and 'cellos, then again catches us out by a sudden shift of key. So sudden that the music itself seems to take offence, for two angry chords cut short any tendency to drift too far afield. With a gesture of extraordinary grace, Schubert readmits us to the strangely elusive world of F major, and rounds off his exposition. The melting final phrase:

Ex.158

was a last-minute inspiration which only appears in his fair copy of the movement.

Because it is a sonata, Schubert seems to have felt that the exposition should be repeated, though few pianists share his view. But to have started once more after so quiet a conclusion would hardly have been effective; some change of mood was needed. He introduced a new, restless little figure, toyed mysteriously with the last three chords of Ex. 158, then suddenly startled his audience out of their wits with a great thunderclap, the only time that that distant rumble which had lent such an individual colour to the first theme is allowed to reveal its latent power.

With a typical stroke of magic, Schubert wafts us gently into C♯ minor[1] at the start of the development. Our ears have been sated perhaps with an overdose of B♭, E♭ and F; how like him then to move into a key in which these notes cannot really be said to appear. It opens the door to even remoter worlds, 'sharp' keys which have only been visited briefly, if at all, during the exposition.

There can be no finer example of Schubert's highly individual method of development than this movement. The music gives a deceptive impression of expansiveness, deceptive, because in its unique way it is every bit as concentrated as a Beethoven development. He begins by giving his opening theme a completely new face. Not only is it in the minor for the first time; it has an unforeseen variant, turning it in new directions.

Ex. 159

How subtle is the relationship between the opening notes of the melody and the apparently new continuation; how unexpected too, the process of compression by which Schubert is able to follow this immediately with a reference to Ex. 157,

[1] Also the key of the slow movement: cf. Mozart K.457, p. 46.

originally a remote contrast to the first subject, but now a close neighbour. The fusion accomplished, Schubert is content for the moment to leave it at that. He turns his attention to Ex. 152, the triplet arpeggios. It is hard to uphold the accusation of long-windedness so often levelled at Schubert in the face of such economy; three main subjects in the first fourteen bars of the development is hardly garrulous.

The ingenuity of his construction is remarkable. For some time, he avoids any further reference to what we have presumed to be the most important themes of the movement. The figuration of Ex. 152 continues, continually changing its tonality, supported by a bass which we can be forgiven for supposing to be no more than a conventional prop.

Ex.160

A climax is reached in the key of D♭ major. The music descends to a low D♭, reiterated like a soft drum-beat. It is here that Schubert plays his most unexpected card, a stroke of sheer genius that truly shows he had no further need to look over his shoulder to the towering figure of Beethoven for help. He takes the unobtrusive bass from the first bar of Ex. 160 and transforms it into a theme of the utmost importance.

Ex.161

With relentless inevitability, he builds this theme up, now in the right hand, now in the left. Dissonances increase the tension, the texture thickens, single notes become octaves, rhythms clash. It is the exact centrepoint of the sonata, a summit from which, on both sides, the landscape descends to the pleasant valleys beneath. Few men, on climbing a mountain, would wish to start the journey down at once. It is only natural to stand and gaze. This is exactly what Schubert seems to do; the music becomes curiously static, the harmonies having a strangely modal quality (see Ex. 142a). In the far distance, we hear again that thunder-roll, and it turns our minds once more to the opening theme. It too is affected by the environment; the harmonies belong, one would think, more to Grieg than to Schubert.

Ex.162

This whole central section is one of the marvels of music; it dies away at last to nothingness—complete silence, the memory of thunder still hanging in the air, yet with our hearts filled with the peace of Nature at her most serene. If Beethoven's Pastoral symphony is, as he claimed, 'more an impression of the countryside than an actual painting', I make no apology for making the same observation about this sonata. I am not inventing Schubert's love of nature; here he is, in a letter to his brother, dated 12 September 1825, describing the inner Salzburg valley.

To describe to you the loveliness of that valley is almost im-possible. Think of a garden several miles in extent, with countless castles and estates in it peeping through the trees; think of a river winding through it in manifold twists and turns; think of meadows and fields like so many carpets of the finest colours, then of the many roads tied round them like ribbons; and lastly avenues of enormous trees to walk in for hours, all enclosed by ranges of the highest mountains as far as the eye can reach, as though they were the guardians of this glorious valley; think of all this and you will have a faint conception of its inexpressible beauty.[1]

[1] Otto Erich Deutsch: *Schubert* (trans. Blom): J. M. Dent, 1946

Inexpressible? Perhaps if Schubert felt that words were inadequate, he may have used music, even without openly admitting it.

As if there were not beauty enough in the first movement, Schubert follows it with a serenade-like Andante that, so far as the piano can, matches the sustained perfection of the slow movement of the C major quintet. I cannot believe that any piano of his time can remotely have done justice to it, but the vision is there. The accompaniment sticks to one rhythm and shape, suggesting a softly-played guitar. The melody is like distant voices singing, moving in simple thirds as people do when they harmonize spontaneously. For all its appearance of simplicity, Schubert employs some wonderfully rich harmonies. Ex. 144 gives a tiny sample of a movement that needs no help from me in conveying its message. If there should ever come a day when the machines finally take over, when the composers abdicate all responsibility, when concert-music is pronounced dead, when man has at last grown artistically impotent—on that black day, let someone play this movement to the dying world; at least we would learn again what beauty is.

The Scherzo is a delight of a different kind, quicksilver and delicate, imbued with the wit that Schubert may have learned from Beethoven, but free from any suggestion of the rough, boisterous character that some people find offensive in Beethoven's music. Schubert exploits extreme registers in this movement, the tunes nearly all being conceived as dialogues, as though between a flute and a bassoon. As one might expect, the modulations are marvellously adroit, turning always in unexpected directions. The central Trio is a subtle example of the village-band joke.[1] All the lads are playing quietly except for

---

[1] I know most performers make it sound darkly spiritual, but I see no reason not to admit it to be as entertaining as the rest of the movement. It can still be great music.

old Joe on the tuba, whose isolated notes stand out like discreet farts at the vicarage.

Ex. 163

The joke is the funnier for being handled so erratically; the pattern of the explosive accents is inconsistent. Occasionally old Joe does manage to pop a note in just right, and we can sense that if only he had had a bit more time to practise or had bought a better instrument, all would be well.

It is unusual to find a sonata in which the only movement to be touched by pathos is the finale. (There are those who would say that the slow movement is sad; but if it is sadness, it is of that nostalgic kind which is a sort of self-indulgence. So much of it is in the major that I refuse to believe that it contains any hint of true grief, such as we found in Beethoven's Op. 110.) The last movement is characterized by a curious inability to stay in the major. Time after time Schubert tries to get into a major key, but it won't 'take'. The movement begins with a single octave G, like two orchestral horns, a note that commands our attention without violence. A little tune begins, Mozartean in style almost, touched with that same pathetic urgency that is so haunting at the start of Mozart's G minor symphony. It is clearly in C minor, even though, with typical deftness, Schubert turns it towards B♭ major.

Ex. 164

That reappearance of the first note is more than just a repetition; it is a denial of B♭ major. A few bars later, the music does seem to have established a successful hold on B♭, but again it is diverted, this time to G minor. Back comes the first little tune again, and as before, it reaches for B♭ major. No sooner is the rightful key for the movement established for the third time than the music drops strangely into A♭ major. This new tonality lasts for a matter of seconds before it too is sabotaged and pushed towards G minor; the crisis is averted, a clever twist taking us back to the elusive B♭. There is a flutter of unease, and the 'horn-call' pulls us away once more into C minor.

It would be laborious to analyse the whole movement in these terms, but I have done enough to draw attention to the curious ambivalence that prevails. Tunes have a habit of ending up in the 'wrong' key. One long sustained theme, whose smooth appearance is belied by the strange off-beat notes that accompany it in the bass, actually starts a phrase in F major and finishes it in D, which might be described as 'a proper turn-up'.

Ex. 165

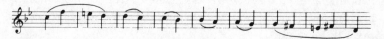

Nothing in this movement seems to behave predictably. The loudest storm emerges out of a total silence; the strongest, most dramatic theme is transformed into something gossamer, delicate as Titania dancing on a moonbeam; a passage that looks as though it is all storming heroics has to be played right against nature, making a continuous diminuendo where one wants to batter the keyboard. If ever a movement deserved the soubriquet Caprice, this is it. Even the ending revels in contradiction; Ex. 164 unfolds for the last time, ambiguous to the end; there is a silence: suddenly, without warning, we are swept away in a torrent of octaves. Is there a suggestion of impatience, of anger even? No: the movement ends joyously, its pathetic opening resolved at last.

I have tried to ride the uneasy precipice between technical jargon and fulsome rhapsody in this analysis; it is difficult to avoid either in a work which combines the mature skill of a craftsman with the divine instinct of an artist to such a degree. It *is* important to understand the intricacies of modulation and key-relationships in classical music, and there is no avoiding the issue. Analysis can only take us so far, and if the end-product of analysis is to make the music less appealing, it has failed utterly. In his *Essays and Lectures on Music*,[1] Donald Tovey has two brilliant chapters on Schubert, the second of which is highly technical, being full of those near-algebraical symbols ($\flat$VI, $\sharp$vi, etc.) that take music into the esoteric realms so dear to the academic mind. He devotes a good deal of space to this sonata, exposing its harmonic bones to the naked eye, if not to the un-trained ear. But—and it is a big 'but'—he ends his chapter with what might be described as a perfect cadence when he says:

> Schubert's tonality is as wonderful as star clusters, and a verbal description of it as dull as a volume of astronomical tables. But I have often been grateful to a dull description that faithfully guides me to the places where great artistic experiences await me . . . .

Tovey had a scholarship to which I could never begin to

[1] Oxford University Press, 1949.

aspire, but even at his most professorial, he preserves a proper scepticism about the theoretician's approach. To give a detailed analysis of the last three sonatas of Schubert would need a book in itself—and a very dreary book it would be. I have tried to say enough to make you realize something of their wonder. Did ever a man spend four weeks of his life bequeathing so much pleasure to mankind?

CHAPTER XI

LISZT

Sonata in B Minor

Composed 1852–3. Dedicated to Schumann. Surprisingly there is no opus number, but Liszt was haphazard and prolific with his compositions, which number over 700. A set of three early sonatas, written in 1825, was lost or destroyed, as was a sonata for piano duet written in the same year. His only other extant sonata is No. 7 of the second set of 'Années de Pèlerinage' (Italie) which is described as 'Après une lecture du Dante, Fantasia quasi Sonata'. It is too much a 'programme' work to be classified as a sonata in the accepted sense of the word.

To follow Schubert with Liszt may seem something of a stylistic gaffe, but there is more logic in it than first meets the eye. Liszt was a great admirer of Schubert's Wanderer Fantasy, a work which he transcribed with excellent taste, making it into a concerto by adding an orchestral part. Its form, which imposes unity on a long work by making some themes common to all four movements, impressed him enormously. (Berlioz had used the same idea, though in a rather more naïve way, in the Fantastic symphony.) It was to become a widely used device during the second half of the nineteenth century, appealing to composers as different in style as Tchaikovsky, César Franck, Wagner and Liszt himself. It can hardly be a coincidence that he should have made his transcription of the Wanderer Fantasy the year before he wrote this sonata. Schubert seems to have given him the clue he was seeking, and his subsequent solution to the problem of how to give sonata form a new look is one of the most significant landmarks in musical history.

Personal taste weighs very heavily in our assessment of a composer like Liszt; even his most ardent admirers would admit that he does flirt with danger at times, going very near the borderline of vulgarity. (Notice the diplomatically ambiguous nature of that phrase: one can be near a border on either side.) All the same, to dismiss the sonata as meretricious trash, as some critics are prone to do, is carrying prejudice too far. Written in his early forties, not long before he deserted the concert-platform, the sonata was not well received at the time, a fact which at once suggests that it was one of Liszt's best compositions. The truly first-rate seldom receives universal critical claim. One must take into account Liszt's position when he was at the height of his career. He was the 'lion' of the century and the leaders of society fought to have the privilege of welcoming him into their homes. Audiences were hungry for sensation at all costs, and Liszt's phenomenal virtuosity could supply it. For him to play an entirely simple piece was to deprive them of their meat and drink; to write a sonata without virtuosity entering into it would have been unthinkable to such a man. Under the circumstances, it is remarkable that he produced a work that is astonishingly inventive in its construction, and truly revolutionary in form. Despite his indebtedness to Schubert for the idea, Liszt was to employ a very different method. The cross references that we find in the Wanderer Fantasy are retrospective; in other words, a theme that has been thoroughly established in the first movement will appear as a reminiscence in the scherzo. Schubert himself probably took the idea from Beethoven's fifth symphony, where the scherzo theme makes a ghostly reappearance in the finale. (It is doubtful whether either Beethoven or Schubert would have known the relatively early symphony by Haydn in which that most inventive composer had already tried the experiment.) Liszt's approach was far more radical. In fact a much later composer, Sibelius, is usually given the credit for inventing the form that Liszt uses in this sonata, just as Debussy is usually credited with inventing the whole-tone scale—a device Liszt was using with assurance when the French composer was still a student.

The very first page proclaims the Revolution. Instead of

the long-established tradition of joining first and second subjects
by a bridge passage, Liszt gives us three ideas, separated from one
another by silences, and seemingly quite unrelated. It's as though
a lecturer were to say, 'Tonight I am going to talk to you about
horses, eggs and trees'. On the face of it, this doesn't look like a very
promising evening, but by the end of it you have been convinced
that horses live in trees and lay eggs. A work lasting nearly half
an hour has been built from a few fragments; the apparently
irreconcilable has been fused together; the insanity of the opening
is revealed as a masterstroke. I doubt if there is any other work
in musical history that is so concentrated in its use of material,
apart from Bach's Musical Offering or the Art of Fugue. Since
both of these are by way of being contrived demonstrations of
particular and limited skills, they are hardly fair comparisons.
In the whole sonata there are only five themes, which could all be
jotted down on the back of a postcard and still leave room for a
message to Mother.

The sonata begins unpromisingly with a couple of isolated
notes followed by a slow descending scale. The two notes are
repeated; the scale descends again, picking its way a little more
carefully; two notes; silence.

Ex.166

We wait expectantly; suddenly, out of the blue, with the
dramatic impact of a Nijinsky leaping onto the stage, theme no. 2
arrives.

Ex.167

Another silence; then, deep down in the most menacing register of the keyboard, comes a fateful knocking, a theme of extraordinary compressed energy.

Ex.168

A quick glance at these three examples shows that in effect, each one consists of a phrase that is stated twice, albeit with some modification. Liszt could hardly make things more compact, yet he is careful to impress these themes upon our minds by this repetition. He has preserved the idea that lay behind the classical convention of repeating the exposition, realizing that it still had a function; but he has reduced it to the barest minimum, and, by choosing themes of so clearly defined individuality, he has made it that much easier for the listener to retain them in his mind.

If we are to explore this sonata in detail, I am going to have to quote these three examples so often that it will be simpler to identify them by name. Let us call Ex. 166 the 'scales' theme, or I, Ex. 167 the 'octave' theme, or II and Ex. 168 the 'knocking' theme, or III. The ingenuity with which Liszt manipulates them, changing their emotional content and continually establishing new relationships between them, is something that gives me as much pleasure now as it did when I first heard the work as a student. There is no better way of discovering just how adaptable musical motifs can be than by observing Liszt at work.

After the very theatrical presentation of his three main ideas, there is a brief silence, as well there might be after such shock tactics. Out of this silence emerges a figure of great agitation:

Ex.169

agitato

Liszt repeats this several times, raising the pitch step by step
in the sort of sequence that some critics would suggest (with some
justification) to be a bit glib. The fact is that it is so effective a way
of whipping up excitement that it has become a cliché, debased
by overmuch use. In 1852 it was more than enough to set pulses
racing. Morever, it is the first of the many transformations we are
to experience. Sounding like a completely new idea, it actually
proves to be derived from Ex. 167, the 'octave' theme. The stages
are easy to see:

Ex.170

(Ex.167, bars 5-6)   = start of Ex.169

At the height of this first climax, the octave theme returns,
harmonized for the first time with a full-blooded chord of E♭
major, while its descending tail streams out like a comet. More
dramatically still, the knocking theme thunders out in the bass
once more as the music settles for the first time into the tonic key
of B minor. It is a moment to store in one's mind, for although
this vast one-movement sonata is constructed on such original
lines, it also pays considerable tribute to traditional form. Some
twenty-five pages further on, a recapitulation in the classical sense
is destined to appear. It starts at the point we have now reached;
according to conventional analysis then, all that we have heard so
far has been a prologue, an announcement of the *dramatis personae*.
The exposition proper begins.

At once a battle is joined between the second and third themes.

II has its tail twisted to some purpose, III hammers away in opposition.

Again the sequences pile up until a summit is reached; down we plunge into a strange turbulence, the rhythm violently disturbed by agitated syncopations. For all its appearance of violent conflict, Liszt's concentration on the matter in hand is extraordinary. The innocent ear could be forgiven for assuming that here, at least, some new material is being used, but Ex. 172a proves how wrong we are.

Out of all the excitement, the octave theme emerges triumphant; even here, Liszt finds a new way of presenting it, making the phrase overlap itself.

This develops into a tremendous passage in octaves, virtuoso music certainly, but evolved legitimately from what has gone before. It finally climbs down on to an A♮ which hammers away relentlessly. Two staccato bass-notes draw our attention to the left hand. A distorted version of the scale theme (I) appears, casting a shadow that makes us quickly forget the heroics of the previous page. Yet even this phrase must be used constructively. Liszt is preparing for a grand entrance, the first appearance of the fourth of the five themes that are all he allows himself in the whole of this sonata.[1] An enormous sense of expectancy is aroused by his ingenious treatment of I, which soon drags itself out of the sepulchral depths and quickens its step.

Ex.174

At last the Grande Dame appears, making a truly royal entrance. Pulsating chords flood our ears with harmony, and one can imagine the magisterial authority Liszt would have brought to such a passage. Of course it is theatrical, more than life-size; but it was written in an age when cynicism had not eroded belief in grandiloquence.

Ex.175

This noble theme, which I shall call IV, is dismantled by the composer after it has run its course; the four notes marked ⌐‾‾‾⌐ are the subject of a brief argument about tonality which ultimately comes to rest on a widespread, expressive chord which turns out

[1] By conventional analysis, it would presumably be termed the 'second' subject, though a more misleading term for the fourth main theme would be hard to find.

to be that old stand-by, a diminished seventh. From this moment of repose, the octave theme (II) reappears, utterly transformed.

There is an interesting point to be raised here about the whole question of musical 'language'. A purist, like Stravinsky, argues that music is something so complete in itself that to use words like 'grand', 'tempestuous', 'tender', 'sad', 'happy' to describe a theme is misleading. He has claimed that, 'by its nature, music is essentially powerless to express anything at all, whether a feeling, an attitude of mind, a psychological attitude, a natural pheno-menon, etc. .... If music seems to express something, this is merely an illusion and not a reality. It is simply an additional attribute which, by tacit and inveterate agreement, we have lent it, thrust upon it, as a label, a convention.'[1] Harsh words from the composer of such vividly descriptive scores as Firebird or Petrushka.

In a way, this sonata, for all its romantic appearance, could be said to bear out Stravinsky's contention. It is almost irresistible to describe theme II as 'heroic', theme III as 'menacing' or theme IV as 'grandiloquent'. Indeed, I am positive that Liszt meant us to think of them in this way. But if I take a *word* like menacing, I cannot give it another meaning, any more than I am likely to make the words 'I love you' convincing by shouting them in anger. (I realize it is possible to imagine a situation in which a man, exasperated by a girl's indifference, might end by yelling, 'Can't you see that I love you!', but it is an unnatural interpretation of the words, affected by an accumulation of events leading up to the particular moment.) I myself have often argued that a musical phrase has a certain emotion built-in to it; to deny the emotional power of music is as foolish as it would be to suggest that a funeral march could be mistaken for a waltz. The fact remains (and this sonata gives a vivid demonstration of its validity) that while we may not be able to change the meaning of a word, we can certainly change the meaning of a musical pattern. Can I suggest a middle road, not so uncompromisingly dispassionate as Stravinsky's,

[1] See Eric Walter White: *Stravinsky*, p. 93: John Lehmann, 1947.

but equally not so governed by sentimentality as are the reactions of the listener who merely uses music as a sort of drug.

In the battle-scenes of his wonderful film version of *Henry V*, Laurence Olivier was clad in armour, riding a white horse. His stirring call of 'Cry God for Harry, England and Saint George!' was delivered at the top of his voice. That he wears doublet and hose and uses gentle tones when paying court to Katherine, the French Princess, does not mean that he is no longer the same man, but only that we are seeing a different aspect of the same man. Thus when we find theme II presented with all the expressive beauty of a Chopin nocturne, it does not mean that it is no longer the same theme. Liszt would be dismayed if we failed to realize that it was, since the idea of transforming the theme is fundamental to his concept. This leads us to the conclusion that it is not the theme itself, but its treatment or presentation that is decisive. Volume, tempo, instrumental timbre, harmonization and, regrettably, standards of performance all have a part to play in deciding our reaction—though a bad performance can only obscure the quality of greatness, not destroy it.

Notes in themselves are virtually meaningless; about the most you can say is that they are high or low, and even that is only relative; the lowest note on the flute is very high for a double bass. Even a sequence of notes as sacrosanct as the theme from the opening movement of the Moonlight sonata is far from absolute in meaning. Suppose that I present them in this way:

Ex.176

The notes are unaltered, yet nobody would suggest that the meaning had not changed. The emotional effect of a composition is due to a wide range of factors, of which melody is, surprisingly, far less important than we imagine. It seems a suitable moment to return to Liszt.

The new version of II, 'tenderized' as the tele-commercials might say, is a reverse application of the technique I have just demonstrated on Beethoven's Op. 27 No. 2. Liszt helps the imperceptive by reminding them of II, presenting it as a single line of unsupported melody, slow and quiet, but with its melodic outline unaltered. He has paved the way for a remarkable change of character:

Ex.177

A visual comparison with Ex. 167 reveals both the similarities and the differences. Tempting though it must have been for Liszt to dally in this dream-world, he soon reminds us that this is not a rhapsody but a sonata by re-introducing III, whose menace is only partly lessened by being played quietly. Yet this theme too, which one would have thought too powerful and compact to be susceptible to much alteration, is transformed.

Ex.178

The supporting harmonies have a faint suggestion of the famous A♭ Liebesträum, written a couple of years earlier,[1] but

_____

[1] Actually a piano transcription of a song composed about 1845.

this could well have been the sort of private cross-reference between works that Schumann enjoyed making (namely Papillons-Carnaval), and the dedication to Schumann suggests the possibility that Liszt had some ulterior motive of an amicable kind. Needless to say the tune is beautifully laid-out for keyboard with some cunning division between the hands. A rising chromatic scale leads us to one of the most magical touches; theme II, having been both heroic and sentimental, now becomes delicate and capricious.

Ex.179

Liszt toys with it for some time, the right hand meanwhile dazzling us with exquisitely wrought patterns that are typical of his keyboard mastery. Just at the moment when virtuosity is beginning to get the upper hand, Ex. 178 puts in an appearance, all sentiment cast aside. Even the most beautiful girl can have a temper, as Liszt would have been the first to know. A soft answer turneth away wrath however, and theme II duly gives it.

Ex.180

Two finely spun candenzas bring us back to a much more dramatic mood, and theme II re-assumes its original heroic attitude, a new figure of brilliant ascending octaves in the left hand intensifying the contrast. For a couple of pages, the storm beats about our heads, although, for all the sound and fury, Liszt keeps an iron control on the material, everything being derived from II.

Sudden storms often bring sunshine in their wake, and so it is now when Liszt causes the music to dissolve into delicately shimmering figuration of the most decorative kind. Almost unbelievably, II is still present in yet another guise.

Ex.181

Having enjoyed himself with a dazzling display of keyboard writing that never loses sight of musical values, for all its glitter, he now brings back Ex. 178 in a still more dramatic version. It leads to one of the most technically daunting pages in the sonata, with fearsome skips in the left hand. At the climax, the scales theme, which has been absent for some time, re-appears in a form more violent than we would have suspected was possible from so reticent a beginning.

Ex.182

All the themes are being thrown together with increasing violence; II returns in its original form, though transposed into a different key; IV presents an entirely different face to the world, no longer a Grande Dame, but an Amazonian Queen ordering a slave to be executed. Despite the savage ferocity of these phrases, we gain the impression that the music is gradually losing momentum. Liszt, whose sense of overall proportion has never deserted him, is preparing the way for what, in effect, is a miniature slow movement. We are very near to the exact centre of the work; the composer is giving us a forcible reminder of the three main components before he bids them a temporary farewell. The knocking theme (III) returns twice in its original form, the first three notes of the octave theme are hurled at us in chunky chords before, remarkably, II and III are combined, a marriage which has not even been hinted at since they were first flung into violent opposition in Ex. 171.

Ex.183

At last, on the nineteenth page of a forty-page work, the
only remaining theme of the five makes its long-delayed appearance. As I have said, it serves the function of a slow movement,
yet this gives the misleading impression that the first four themes
are now going to be put aside. For a time we might well imagine
this to be the case as this new and very Wagnerian melody casts
its spell.

Ex.184 = Ⅴ

(Andante sostenuto)

'Casts its spell' is right, for soon themes III and IV find themselves
in this new environment, and are deeply affected by it. Some
traces of the Amazonian severity that had so transformed IV still
linger, but the general tone is lyrical, whether tender or
passionate.

A sustained increase in tone brings us to the re-emergence of II,
now plunging into unaccustomed depths, but in the end it is the
new theme, V, that dominates this central section. Liszt's use of
slow descending scales is particularly ravishing here, recalling
something of the serene simplicity that we find in the slow
movement of Beethoven's Emperor concerto—a work he must

have played many times. The slow movement, as we may legitimately think of it, ends with two solemn reminders of the scale theme, (I), virtually unaltered from its original version apart from a change of key. The music dies away to silence.

Counterpoint and fugue are not the first two words that spring to mind when we think of Liszt; however, we should remember his enormous admiration for Bach, and the magnificent transcriptions he made of a number of Bach's organ works. He was so gifted that he could turn his hand successfully to most things, and he now has the sense to realize that our aural palate is in danger of having been glutted by a surfeit of sweetness. Something cerebral is needed by way of contrast. In a moment of sheer inspiration, he embarks on a fugue, a muted, diabolical sort of fugue, such as Mephistopheles might have given a lazy student to practise as punishment for past sins. II and III are interwoven with uncanny facility. It is more complicated to describe than to witness; here, then, are some of the fusions of the two ideas.

Ex.185

Ex.185a

Gradually out of this bustling counterpoint the original outlines of II and III begin to re-establish themselves more and more solidly.

Ex.186

But Liszt's ingenuity is by no means exhausted. The music sounds as though it is driven onwards with inhuman energy, yet in fact it is growing increasingly cerebral. The next step is to 'invert' II, turning it upside down.

Ex.187

This is a common enough trick even in the most academic of fugues; what is not so common is to fit a fugue subject against itself in yet another version. It needed genius to spot this opportunity, especially in the heat of such a moment. Here is the newly modified version of II:

Ex.188

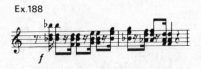

it will be found to fit perfectly against the first two bars of the previous example. This 'battle-in-Looking-Glass-land' is sustained for some time until once again II emerges triumphant (as heroes should); lightning flashes, thunder rolls, and suddenly we are plunged into the recapitulation that I prophesied on p. 157.

It is these classical landmarks within such a novel landscape that make this sonata such an outstanding achievement. However, they bring an interesting comparison to light. Aware as he must have been that he was running the risk of losing control of a work conceived on such a huge scale, Liszt not only felt the need for some vestiges of classical discipline, but, paradoxically, put music into a far tighter straitjacket than it had been in for years. The loosening-up process initiated by Beethoven and continued by Schubert could be said to have been carried on by Liszt in so far as much of the work is revolutionary in concept. But just as political revolutions prompted by a desire for freedom often result in worse tyrannies, so did this musical revolution result in a tightening of control. The extraordinary concentration on a very small amount of musical material that is the hallmark of this sonata is the antithesis of Romanticism. It is a concentration comparable to that which we find in the first movement of Beethoven's fifth symphony, even though the work itself seems to belong to a totally different world of indulgent excess. An exactly parallel situation is to be found at the start of the twentieth century—the revolution accomplished by Schoenberg, aiming at a new freedom, resulted in the most repressive and total discipline ever imposed on music, serialism.

Liszt's recapitulation contains a number of new features, as good recapitulations should; most of them are clearly recognizable, though one ingenious compression of the octave theme deserves mention.

Ex.189

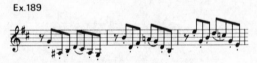

This is later developed into a notoriously difficult octave passage in B major which is a cruel hurdle to place so near to the end of one of the most daunting technical challenges in the repertoire. Surprisingly though, the work ends quietly. After the ultimate supreme climax in terms of volume and physical effort, there is a long silence, out of which theme V emerges like a benediction. The final page is an inspiration; eight times we hear the knocking theme grumbling away in the bass as enigmatic harmonies rise slowly towards the upper reaches of the keyboard. The quietest and most contemplative version of II that has appeared so far gives way to a few solemn chords. We begin to realize that

Liszt is reviewing the material for the last time, in the reverse order to that in which it first appeared (III—II—I). The slow descending scales of I make their way down to the lowest C on the keyboard, the bottom note but one. On this note, so near to the tonic (B), Liszt pauses tantalizingly. It lingers in our minds as he places first a chord of A minor (which is related to C♮) then F major (also related to C) then, three times, the chord of B major, which is totally foreign to C. By now the low C is scarcely audible; but it remains hanging in the air, an infinitely subtle irritant that prevents the three B major chords from giving us a sense of true finality. At last, after one of the longest pauses in music, the tension is released with a soft touch on the bottom B. It is a marvellous exploitation of the benefits of a tonal system. Yet it was Liszt, more than any other figure in the nineteenth century, who was the first to foresee the possibility of that system breaking down. As an old man, he wrote some remarkably prophetic pieces, anticipating developments in harmony and musical thinking that were to take another thirty years to come to fruition. With the collapse of tonality, the backbone of sonata form was broken; we shall see in the next and last chapter a work which, like this one, strives to bring classical disciplines to revolutionary ideas; unlike this, it stands on the very brink of a period when the entire tonal system was on the point of disintegration.

Liszt never wrote another sonata, but plenty more sonatas were written, mostly for more than one instrument. In some way, composers seem to have felt that the possibilities of dialogue between two players would prove more productive. During the twentieth century, the piano itself has suffered a certain devaluation as a solo instrument;[1] increasingly, composers have come to regard it as a sophisticated member of the family of tuned percussion. Over the whole history of music, its period of supremacy was comparatively short; perhaps the reason for its decline was the extraordinary inventiveness and mastery that Liszt, Chopin, Schumann and Brahms showed in handling an instrument that provided their most personal and satisfying mode of expression.

---

[1] We are currently witnessing a similar decline in interest in the standard symphony orchestra; composers want to use combinations of sound that are less hallowed by tradition.

CHAPTER XII

ALBAN BERG
Sonata Op. 1

Composed 1907–8. Published 1910, but twice revised, in 1920 and 1927. First performance on 24 April 1911, together with the String Quartet Op. 3. Originally planned as three-movement sonata, but Berg found difficulty in composing the other movements. On the advice of his teacher, Schoenberg, he decided to accept that the work was complete as it stood.

WAGNER'S EARLIEST LISTED WORK, written in 1829, was a piano sonata. He was to follow this with two more (one for four hands), but they are student works which reveal nothing of his true musical personality. It is tempting to say that the Sonata Op. 1, by Alban Berg, is the sonata Wagner might have written had he lived a few more years, and, in his old age, wished to turn back to a medium he had neglected entirely since his student days in Leipzig. (He took lessons with the cantor of the very church at which J. S. Bach had been organist a century before.) The Berg sonata is enormously influenced by Wagner; but since Wagner and Liszt shared many of the same ideas about music, it seems logical to follow the Liszt sonata with a brief analysis of this work. Three quotations alone should be enough to establish a mutual relationship between the three composers. Here, first, is the main theme of Liszt's Faust symphony, unquestionably his finest orchestral work.

Ex.190

Lento assai

This remarkable work was composed in 1854: in the same year, Wagner began his opera, Die Walküre, which, not surprisingly, took the best part of two years to compose. In the second act we find this theme:[1]

Ex.191

One of the most important motifs in the Berg sonata, as we shall see, is a very near relative to the last three notes of bars 1 and 2 of Ex. 190. The similarity of style is most easily identified in this passage from the start of the development; compare the left hand with Ex. 190.

Ex.192

The Faust symphony theme, Ex. 190, has been often cited as evidence of the historical inevitability of Schoenberg's method of composing, treating all twelve notes of the chromatic scale as equal. It is perfectly true that bars 1 and 2 of Ex. 190 contain the twelve chromatic notes presented in such a way as to give no definition of key. No harmony made up of any of the three-note patterns is explicable in terms of classical tonality. Of course the textbooks have a name for them (augmented triads) but that does not explain their function, which is to be 'no-man's-land' chords. As has been suggested in the previous chapter, the whole tonal basis of music was beginning to disintegrate around the turn

[1] For other equally intriguing parallels between Liszt and Wagner, see Humphrey Searle: *The Music of Liszt*: Williams & Norgate, 1954.

of the century. If conventional harmonies were used, they were often combined in such a way as to disguise their true nature, as Stravinsky did in Petrushka when he combined the arpeggios of C major and F♯ major, both of them pillars of orthodoxy, but here presented in close juxtaposition.

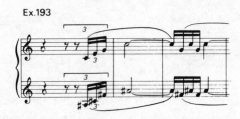

Ex.193

Even such violent oppositions of tonality as this had been anticipated by Liszt in such late piano pieces as Unstern, at whose climax we find chords of astonishing dissonance.

(Although this is a good deal more complex harmonically than the Stravinsky example above, it could be interpreted on rather similar lines if we think of it as a combination of chords of C major and E major, both of them knocked out of shape by the violence of the collision.)

I have no intention of embarking on a long explanation of the conclusions Schoenberg reached after fifteen years of intensive thought, conclusions that led to what might be termed an entirely new grammar and syntax for the expression of musical thought. All I have tried to do in this brief introduction is to establish the situation in which Berg and his contemporaries found themselves in the first decade of the twentieth century. To those who continue to bewail the loss of tonality in music I would just offer one reminder; every one of the great revolutionaries who changed the course of music during this era, Schoenberg, Stravinsky, Bartók, Debussy, Hindemith, started by writing tonal music that acknowledged their inheritance from the great Romantic era that preceded them. Each one came to the same conclusion, not as a result of attending a conference in Margate in 1910 where a resolution was passed saying, 'Let's all write beastly music that nobody will like', but because they found that the language of the post-Wagner era was no longer a valid one. The historical interest of the Berg sonata, which justifies its inclusion here, is that it is a perfect symbol of the state of flux into which music was drifting at the time.

Just as Liszt had to impose severe disciplines on a work that could easily have seemed disorganized, so does Berg fall back on classical procedures. The sonata clearly has an Exposition (repeated in the tradition established so long before), a Development, and a Recapitulation. Instead of two subjects, it has three, which in the original edition he obligingly labelled with their own tempi—tempo I, tempo II, and tempo III. These labels were subsequently dropped, since Berg must have realized the essential contradiction of identifying a theme by its tempo when the tempo itself was subject to continuous change. Admittedly he begins with the instruction 'Mäßig bewegt', or Allegro Moderato in more conventional terms; but as we can see in this next example, there are only two beats before the speed begins to change.

Ex.194

It is interesting to see that although Berg gives the sonata a key-signature of B minor, he seems to have so little faith in the power of tonality that he plasters the score with gratuitous accidentals,[1] in case the performer should be in doubt as to his intentions. Even in the brief extract shown here, there are fourteen accidentals that are not strictly necessary, since they are already covered by the key-signature. It is obvious from this that although Berg acknowledges tonality, he isn't really *thinking* tonally. As to the instruction '*a tempo*' in the fourth full bar, a cynic might be tempted to ask, '*a* what *tempo*?', since so far all we have had has been an accelerando and a ritardando.

This continual fluctuation of speed continues through the next phrase which involves two more bars of getting quicker followed by a long drawn-out retardation, which in turn is replaced by a new tempo, faster than the opening one. Now contrasts of tempo are nothing new; we find them brilliantly exploited in late Beethoven, and in the Liszt sonata we saw him presenting three themes at three different speeds on the very first page. The continuous *variation* of tempo that we find in the Berg sonata is something very different; it injects a feverish quality into the music. One feels that emotion is being conveyed at a very 'physical' level, no longer subject to the controls which are still to be observed in the music of Beethoven, Mozart or Bach, even when they are at their most expressive. The influence of 'Tristan' is very powerful, not only in terms of musical texture, but also in musical purpose— the expression of sensuousness and eroticism in music.

The stage is set for a conflict, then, between the expressive force of the music and the essentially intellectual mould into which the youthful[2] composer has chosen to pour his ideas, rather as if a man had agreed to play three simultaneous games of chess at a championship level while making passionate love to his mistress. Time and again in this sonata one feels that the emotion is overtaxing the structure; the indication of *ffff* is qualified a

---

[1] Accidentals are the signs for natural, sharp, or flat: ♮, ♯, ♭; also double sharp or double flat: 𝄪, ♭♭.

[2] In his early twenties.

bar later by the reservation 'always expressive'. During the course of eight consecutive bars near the end, we find these instructions to the player:

> *ff.* Broader. Quickening again. Broader. Quickening again.
> *fff.* Expressive. Very expressive. Getting quieter and slower.
> Continually expressive. (Getting quieter and slower.)

together with fifteen symbols of ◁ and ▷, and sixteen notes specifically marked with accents.

Opposed to this extreme outpouring of emotion is the notable discipline of the structure itself. The music may seem to be built on very shifting ground from the point of view of tonality, but there is hardly a note that cannot be regarded as relevant to one or other of the three subjects. Even the subjects themselves are subtly related. We have already seen the first subject in Ex. 194. A subsidiary version appears as early as the eleventh bar, by which time we have already experienced a substantial climax followed by a dying fall that takes us down to *pp*. It is what I have sometimes called 'a little death', and from it, Berg lifts us up once more.

Ex.195

The essential orchestral and contrapuntal nature of Berg's thought is clearly revealed by the extreme care that has gone into the notation. The left hand chords in bars 3 and 4 are not thought of as chords at all; having devised a canon between the two hands, he continues to think in terms of interweaving lines of melody whose identity must be preserved. This explains the eccentric notation of what a pianist would think of as a perfectly ordinary fifth in the fourth bar.[1]

The rising triplet marked  is enormously important, sprouting persistently through the texture like a fast-growing plant. Berg soon reveals its relationship to the first subject when he replaces the opening three notes of Ex. 194

with this substitute from Ex. 195.

Ingenuities of construction are so frequent that it would be unnecessarily arduous to point them all out; their purpose is to impose unity as much as to develop, and this they succeed in doing admirably. A typical example is the way that Berg arrives at his third subject. A characteristic climax has flared up, sparked off by what seems to be little more than a romantic gesture of the head-tossing kind.

Ex.196

[1] Compare Beethoven, Op. 110, Ex. 124.

(Notice again that there is a canon between the two hands.)

This agitated pattern continues to erupt from time to time in a slightly compressed form:

Ex.196a

gradually dying down until it emerges in a transformation Liszt himself would have been proud to have devised.

Ex.197
(Much slower)

A quick glance at the second bar will show how easy it is for Berg to find his way back from this theme to the opening subject (Ex. 194).

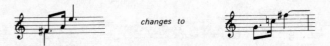

changes to

The second subject, which I have so far only mentioned, is also linked to the first, since both themes begin with the same rhythm ♫♩. Where one rises, the other falls.

Ex.198
(Slower than Tempo I)

ritard.

espr.

Here, again, we have the contradiction of music of extreme sensuousness wearing academic dress; the fragment 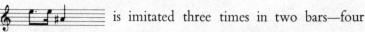 is imitated three times in two bars—four times, if we include the augmented version 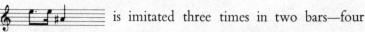.

Although the harmonic texture is almost too rich, Berg is continuing to 'think' entirely in counterpoint; the three-fold repetition of the ♮ symbol on the note A in bar 2 is clear evidence that in his mind, the note is played by a different 'instrument' each time.

The brevity of this sonata, a mere eleven pages, is amply compensated for by the concentration of the material, and the tremendous intensity of emotion. The ending is hauntingly beautiful, a long-drawn-out cadence, intellectually strengthened by the bass (which is an inversion of Ex. 197), while at the same time conveying a sense of exhaustion that is quite proper in a work that has had more than its share of emotional ups-and-downs.

Ex.199

I have often maintained that the history of music shows composers continually having to find new ways of saying things that have already been said by their predecessors. It is obvious that the simple, direct ways are discovered first; therefore, one can argue with some cogency that musical evolution has enforced an ever-growing complexity upon the creative artist. If a path is well-trodden, it is simply because it is the easiest route to take. I am not in any way belittling Berg's achievement when I say that this dying cadence, in which one can discern the twilight of Romanticism, has been expressed before in infinitely simpler terms by Chopin. Tears are tears, whatever dress the man who sheds them may wear.

Ex.200

Chopin
Op. 28 No.4

INDEX